T0140405

Wireless Networks

Series Editor

Xuemin Sherman Shen, University of Waterloo, Waterloo, ON, Canada

The purpose of Springer's Wireless Networks book series is to establish the state of the art and set the course for future research and development in wireless communication networks. The scope of this series includes not only all aspects of wireless networks (including cellular networks, WiFi, sensor networks, and vehicular networks), but related areas such as cloud computing and big data. The series serves as a central source of references for wireless networks research and development. It aims to publish thorough and cohesive overviews on specific topics in wireless networks, as well as works that are larger in scope than survey articles and that contain more detailed background information. The series also provides coverage of advanced and timely topics worthy of monographs, contributed volumes, textbooks and handbooks.

** Indexing: Wireless Networks is indexed in EBSCO databases and DPLB **

More information about this series at http://www.springer.com/series/14180

Longxiang Gao • Tom H. Luan • Bruce Gu •
Youyang Qu • Yong Xiang

Privacy-Preserving in Edge Computing

 Springer

Longxiang Gao (iD)
School of Information Technology
Deakin University
Burwood, VIC, Australia

Tom H. Luan (iD)
School of Cyber Engineering
Xi'an Dianzi University
Xi'an, Shaanxi, China

Bruce Gu (iD)
College of Engineering and Science
Victoria University
Melbourne, VIC, Australia

Youyang Qu (iD)
School of Information Technology
Deakin University
Melbourne, VIC, Australia

Yong Xiang (iD)
School of Information Technology
Deakin University
Melbourne, VIC, Australia

ISSN 2366-1186   ISSN 2366-1445   (electronic)
Wireless Networks
ISBN 978-981-16-2201-4   ISBN 978-981-16-2199-4   (eBook)
https://doi.org/10.1007/978-981-16-2199-4

This Springer imprint is published by the registered company Springer Nature Singapore Pte Ltd.
The registered company address is: 152 Beach Road, #21-01/04 Gateway East, Singapore 189721,
Singapore

Preface

With the rapid development of big data, it is necessary to transfer the massive data generated by end devices to the cloud under the traditional cloud computing model. However, the delays caused by massive data transmission no longer meet the requirements of various real-time mobile services. Therefore, the emergence of edge computing has been recently developed as a new computing paradigm that can collect and process data at the edge of the network, which brings significant convenience to solving problems such as delay, bandwidth, and off-loading in the traditional cloud computing paradigm. By extending the functions of the cloud to the edge of the network, edge computing provides effective data access control, computation, processing, and storage for end devices. Furthermore, edge computing optimizes the seamless connection from the cloud to devices, which is considered the foundation for realizing the interconnection of everything. However, due to the open features of edge computing, such as content awareness, real-time computing, and parallel processing, the existing problems of privacy in the edge computing environment have become more prominent. The access to multiple categories and large numbers of devices in edge computing also creates new privacy issues.

In this book, we discuss on the research background and current research process of privacy protection in edge computing. In the first chapter, the state-of-the-art research of edge computing are reviewed. The second chapter discusses the data privacy issue and attack models in edge computing. Three categories of privacy-preserving schemes will be further introduced in the following chapters. Chapter 3 introduces the context-aware privacy-preserving scheme. Chapter 4 further introduces a location-aware differential privacy-preserving scheme. Chapter 5 presents a new blockchain-based decentralized privacy preserving in edge computing. Chapter 6 summarizes this monograph and proposes future research directions.

In summary, this book introduces the following techniques in edge computing: (1) describes an MDP-based privacy-preserving model to solve context-aware data privacy in the hierarchical edge computing paradigm; (2) describes an SDN-based clustering method to solve the location-aware privacy problems in edge computing; and (3) describes a novel blockchain-based decentralized privacy-preserving scheme in edge computing. These techniques enable the rapid development of privacy preserving in edge computing.

Melbourne, VIC, Australia   Longxiang Gao
Xi'an, China   Tom H. Luan
Melbourne, VIC, Australia   Bruce Gu
Melbourne, VIC, Australia   Youyang Qu
Melbourne, VIC, Australia   Yong Xiang
March 2021

Contents

Acronyms

AP	Affinity propagation
AWGN	Additive white Gaussian noise
CCDF	Complementary cumulative distribution function
CCDP	Classic customizable differential privacy
CDN	Information centric network
CDP	Classic ϵ-differential privacy
CNN	Condensed nearest neighbor
CP-ABE	Ciphertext policy-attribute based encryption
DDoS	Distributed denial-of-service attack
DDSDP	Dynamic dual-scheme ϵ-customized differential privacy
DHT	Distributed hash table
DP	Differential privacy
DSL	Dynamic solution layer
EWM	Entropy weight method
FDMA	Frequency division multiple access
FL	Federated learning
FL-Block	Blockchain-enabled federated learning
GCA	Grid-based clustering algorithm
ICN	Information centric network
IIoTs	Industrial Internet of Things
IoTs	Internet of Things
LTE	Long-term evolution
MDP	Markov decision process
MDP-PPFC	Markov decision process based privacy preserving
NE	Nash equilibrium
PCP	Privacy-preserving content-based publish
PoW	Proof of work
PPFA	Privacy preserving fog-enabled aggregation
QoS	Quality of service

ReLU	Rectified linear unit
SARSA	State action reward state action
SDN	Software defined network
SVRG	Stochastic variance reduced gradient

Chapter 1
An Introduction to Edge Computing

With the continuous development of the Internet of Things (IoTs) [1] applications, such as smart cities and intelligent transportation [2], and the rapid development of location-aware and context-aware services [3], the number of IoTs equipment connections and data generated demonstrate massive growth trends. The traditional cloud computing model adopts a centralized processing mode, which transfers all data to the cloud center through the network. Cloud computing uses powerful computing capabilities to resolve computational and storage problems centrally. Under the background of all interconnected IoTs applications, the characteristics of cloud computing, such as centralized computation, transmission bandwidth, and data privacy [4], become more prominent [5]. The massive data generated by various access devices limit the network bandwidth of cloud computing [6]. These issues cause cloud computing to be overwhelmed and cause greater bottlenecks in the data processing. For example, cloud computing is not compromised with delay-sensitive systems. Delay-sensitive service is usually located at the edge of data center and uses nearby computing equipment to obtain computation and reduce the delay [7]. Data center focused cloud computing has difficulty to meet the demand for low latency focused network architecture and applications. Therefore, edge computing and its applications have arisen and become a research hotspot in recent years.

This monograph introduces edge computing from the networking perspective. We argue that edge computing is dedicated to serving mobile users for engaged location-based applications. By deploying reserved computing and communication resources at the proximity of users, edge computing absorbs the intensive mobile traffic using local fast-rate connections and relieves the long back-and-forth data transmissions among cloud and mobile users. This significantly improves the service quality perceived by users, and more importantly, save both the bandwidth cost and energy consumption. Therefore, edge computing represents a scalable, sustainable, and energy efficient solution to enable the convergence of cloud-based Internet and the mobile computing.

© The Author(s), under exclusive license to Springer Nature Singapore Pte Ltd. 2021
L. Gao et al., *Privacy-Preserving in Edge Computing*, Wireless Networks,
https://doi.org/10.1007/978-981-16-2199-4_1

The purpose of this chapter is to investigate on the major motivation and design goals of edge computing. We emphasize that the emergence of edge computing is motivated by the predictable service demands of mobile users, and edge computing is thus mainly used to fulfill the service requests on localized information. As an edge server possesses hardware resources in three dimensions (storage, computing, and communications), their service-oriented resource allocations are therefore the key of edge computing. Moreover, with the three-tier architecture, mobile-edge-cloud, and rich potential applications in both mobile networking and IoTs, edge computing also opens broad research issues on network management, traffic engineering, big data, and novel service delivery.

While been actively pursued recently, edge computing is still new and lacks a standardized definition. We will provide a definition of edge computing from the networking perspective, with the goal to shape the key features of edge computing and identify its main design goals. In the rest part of this chapter, we will also unfold our journey by first describing the basic system architecture of edge computing, demonstrating advantages of edge computing, and showcasing some exemplary application scenarios.

1.1   Definition of Edge Computing

Edge computing is a new computing paradigm that performs computational capabilities at the edge of network [8]. The idea of edge computing is by placing light-weight cloud-like facility at the proximity of mobile users. The edge computing objects include uplink data from end devices and downlink data from cloud services. Edge computing allows end devices to migrate storage and computing tasks to edge nodes, which not only meets the demand of expanding the computing capacity of end devices but also effectively resolves the transmission link resources between end devices and cloud servers.

The "edge" of edge computing refers to any computing devices and network resources between data sources and cloud computing centers [9]. The edge consists variety range of the devices in edge networks that can be traditional network devices (routers, switches, gateways, etc.) already deployed on the network or local servers that are specifically deployed. Generally, specifically deployed devices have more resources, while traditional network devices with plenty of resources can significantly reduce costs. Both devices have much smaller resource capabilities than a data center, but their large number can compensate for the shortage of a single device. The edge platform consists of a large number of edge nodes and these edge nodes can be dispersed in different geographical locations, in stark contrast to data centers in a resource pool.

The edge therefore can serve mobile users with a direct short-fat wireless connection as compared to the long-thin mobile cloud connection. More importantly, as deployed at specific localized sites, edge computing can provide customized and engaged location-aware services, which are more desirable to mobile users.

1.2   Architecture of Edge Computing

Edge computing extends cloud computing by introducing an intermediate edge layer between mobile devices and cloud. This accordingly leads to a three-layer Mobile-Edge-Cloud hierarchy, where Fig. 1.1 illustrates a brief architecture of edge computing.

The intermediate edge layer is composed of geo-distributed edge servers which are deployed at the local premises of mobile users, e.g., parks, bus terminals, shopping centers, etc. An edge server is a virtualized device with built-in data storage, computing, and communication facility; the purpose of edge computing is therefore to place a handful of compute, storage, and communication resources in the close proximity of mobile users, and accordingly provide fast-rate services to mobile users via the local short-distance high-rate wireless connections. An edge server can be adapted from existing network components, e.g., a cellular base station, WiFi access point or femtocell router, by upgrading the computing and storage resources and reusing the wireless interface. An edge server can be static at a fixed location, e.g., inside a shop installed similarly as a WiFi access point, or mobile placed on a moving vehicle as the Greyhound "BLUE" system [10]. Some exemplary use cases will be discussed in the last section of this chapter.

The role of edge servers is to bridge the mobile users and cloud. On one hand, edge servers directly communicate with mobile users through single-hop wireless connections using the off-the-shelf wireless interfaces, such as WiFi, cellular, or

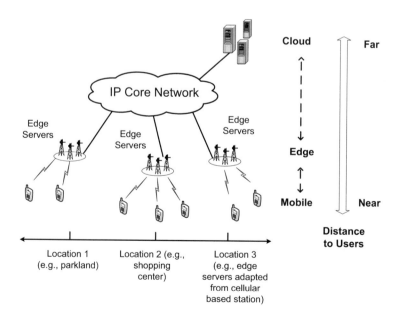

Fig. 1.1 Edge computing architecture

Bluetooth.[1] With cloud-like resources, an edge server is able to independently provide pre-defined application services to mobile users in its wireless coverage without the assistances of other edge servers or remote cloud. On the other hand, the edge servers can be connected to the cloud over Internet so as to leverage the rich computing and content resources of cloud.

To summarize, the edge computing is to deploy the virtualized cloud-like device more close to mobile users, and therefore the edge is interpreted as "the cloud close to the ground" [11]. In what follows, we will discuss on the rationale of edge computing and exhibit some exemplary application scenarios.

Design from Storage, Computing, and Communication Unlike the gateway device in traditional access networks, e.g., WiFi and cellular network, an edge server is a generic virtualized equipment with the on-board storage, computing, and communication capability. Therefore, an edge server is a much more powerful and flexible device managing three-dimensional resources and can deliver more intelligent and adaptive services.

1.2.1   Storage

In a specific service area, an edge server predicts the mobile user's demand on information and pre-caches the most desirable contents accordingly using a proactive way [12]. Such information can be either retrieved from the cloud or uploaded by its owner. For example, the edge servers deployed in the airport can pre-cache the flight and local transportation information which is desirable to travellers in the airport. Therefore, the key design issue of edge computing is to predict the user's demand and proactively select the contents to cache in the geo-distributed edge servers based on the specific locations.

Some existing network storage services and their comparisons with edge specific service are

- The Content Delivery Network (CDN) [13] represents the most mature catch networks and is extensively pursued in both academic and industry. CDN is the Internet-based cache network by deploying cache servers at the edge of Internet to reduce the download delay of contents from remote sites. CDN mainly targets to serve traditional Internet users, which have much broader and unpredictable interests and service demands. In contrast to CDN, with the precise service region, an edge server has much clearer target users and service demand. It is thus key for edge servers to explore the location feature to fully utilize its storage and computing resources to provide the most desirable services to mobile users.

---

[1]Apple has released iBeacon framework in iOS to support edge computing services using Bluetooth.

- Information Centric Network (ICN) [14] is a wireless cache infrastructure which provides content distribution services to mobile users with distributed cache servers. Different from the cache servers in ICN, the edge servers are intelligent computing unit. Therefore, the edge servers are not only used for caching but also as a computing infrastructure to interact with mobile users and devices for real-time data processing. The edge servers can be connected to the cloud and leverage the scalable computing power and big data tools for rich applications other than content distribution, such as Internet of Things, vehicular communications, and smart grid applications [11].
- Baştuğ et al. [12] show that the information demand patterns of mobile users are predictable to an extent and propose to proactively pre-cache the desirable information before users request it. The social relations and device-to-device communications are leveraged. Edge computing is a much more broad and generic paradigm as compared in [12]. The proactive caching framework is desirable and applicable in edge computing.

1.2.2 Computing

A salient feature that differentiates edge computing from the traditional cache networks and access technologies is that edge servers are an intelligent computing system. This allows an edge server to autonomously [15] and independently serve local computation and data processing requests from mobile users. Satyanarayanan et al. [16] shows the applications of edge computing in the cognitive applications. In another example, an edge server inside the shopping mall or scenery park can maintain an on-board geographic information system and provide the real-time navigation and video streaming to connected mobile users.

Bridging the mobile and cloud, an edge server can also be conveniently used to collect the environmental or utility data from mobile users at the deployed spot, and transmit the collected big data to cloud for in-depth data analysis; the results can be provided to third party for strategic and valuable insights on business and government event planning, execution, and measurement.

Despite the high computing power, the cloud is faraway from mobile users and can hardly support real-time computing intensive applications due to the constrained bandwidth of networks. The demand of real-time resource-intensive mobile applications, e.g., cognitive and IoT applications, motivates the design of ubiquitous edge computing system [16, 17]. Cloudlets [16, 18] adopt the same framework of edge computing, in which a Cloudlet server, similar to the edge server, is deployed in the proximity of mobile users and processes the local computing requests of mobile devices at real-time for video streaming and data processing. A comparison of processing delays using Cloudlets and Amazon clouds is shown in http://elijah.cs.cmu.edu/demo.html. The Cloudlets as described in [16, 18] primarily focuses on providing computing services [19]; the Cloudlets, however, can be easily adapted to edge computing. Transparent computing [17] is a highly virtualized system, which targets to develop the computing system transparent to users with cross-platform and cross-application support.

The edge computing is a generic platform for edge computing and, more importantly, edge computing focuses on serving the localized information applications and computation requests. The prototype and techniques in [16, 17] can be incorporated in edge computing framework.

1.2.3   Communication

With the Mobile-Edge-Cloud architecture shown in Fig. 1.1, an edge server maintains three sorts of connections at the same time: wireless connections from the edge server to the local mobile users, wired/wireless connections among peered edge servers, and wired/wireless connections to the cloud, as indicated in Fig. 1.2. For each of these three aspects, we have:

Communications Between Mobile and Edge
An edge server may adopt the off-the-shelf wireless interfaces, e.g., WiFi and Bluetooth, to connect with the mobile users. However, with the application- and

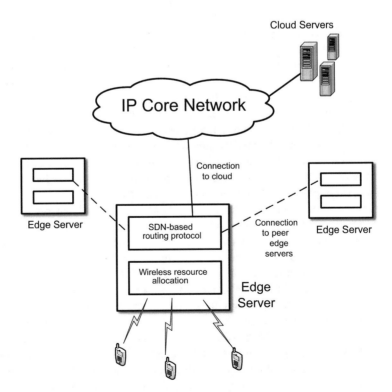

Fig. 1.2 Networking connections of Edge computing

location-awareness, the edge server provides rich potentials for optimal wireless resource allocation from the following two aspects:

Cross-Layer Design Unlike traditional WiFi access points, the edge server manages an autonomous, all-inclusive network by providing both service applications and wireless communications to mobile users in the coverage. Therefore, an edge server can manage all the communication layers and effectively enable the cross-layer design to provide the best service quality to users. For example, as in "BLUE" [10], an edge server can cache a number of videos and deliver YouTube-like video streaming services to mobile users in the proximity. In this case, based on the context, wireless channel, and video popularity information, the video services can be conveniently adapted toward the optimal performance via cross-layer adjustifications.

Predictable User Feature and Demand With specific location, mobile users typically present predictable features and service demand. For example, an edge computing system deployed in the shopping mall needs to address the diverse mobilities of users, whereas the similar system deployed in the inter-state bus [10] only needs to consider static on-board passengers. In addition, the edge computing system in a shopping center may target to serve elastic traffic for ads and sales information delivery, whereas that deployed on a bus may need to target multimedia applications with inelastic traffic. Therefore, an edge server needs to adapt to wireless interface to fully explore the localized user features and service demand.

Communications Between Edge and Cloud
The cloud performs two roles in an edge computing system. First, the cloud is the central controller of edge servers deployed at different locations. With each edge server focusing on the service delivery to mobile users at specific locations, the cloud manages and coordinates the geo-distributed edge servers at different regions. Second, the cloud is the central information depot. The edge servers at different locations select the information contents from the cloud and then deliver the replicas of contents from its cache to the mobile users.

Figure 1.3 shows the software structure of an edge computing system. A cloud server manages the applications and contents for the entire system. At an edge server, selective localized applications are provisioned and synchronized with the cloud.

With the dual functions of cloud, the data delivery and update from cloud to edge can be realized using a software-defined networking (SDN) approach [20]. In this case, the traffic routing is decoupled to the control plane and data plane in which the cloud manages the network with a global view and establishes the routing path of data to update the geo-distributed edge servers.

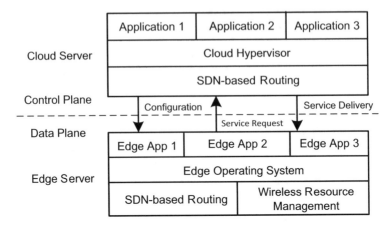

Fig. 1.3 Runtime of edge computing system

Table 1.1 Comparison of edge computing and cloud computing

	Edge computing	Cloud computing
Target user	*Mobile users*	*General Internet users*
Service Type	Limited localized information services related to specific deployment locations	Global information collected worldwide
Hardware	Limited storage, compute power, and wireless interface	Ample and scalable storage space and compute power
Distance to Users	In the physical proximity and communicate through single-hop wireless connection	Faraway from users and communicate through IP networks
Working Environment	Outdoor (streets, parklands, etc.); Indoor (restaurants, shopping malls, etc.)	Warehouse-sized building with air conditioning systems
Deployment	Centralized or distributed in regional areas by local business (local telecommunication vendor, shopping mall retailer, etc.)	Centralized and maintained by Amazon, Google, etc.

Communications Between Edges

An edge server at different locations manages a pool of resources locally. This makes the collaborative service provision and content delivery among peered edge servers promising to improve the entire system performance. The data routing among edge servers can be managed either by a centralized manner using the SDN-based approach or by a fully distributed manner through the traditional routing mechanism, e.g., OSPF. In addition, the data transmission is challenged by the following issues:

- **Service policy**: As shown in Table 1.1 and illustrated in Fig. 1.1, the edge servers at different locations may be deployed by different entities for distinct commercial usages. As a result, they may conform to different policies defined by owners and therefore the data routing among edge servers needs to address the heterogeneous service policies.

- **Topology**: Edge servers co-located in the same region may be connected to the Internet through the same Internet service provider with the high-rate low-cost connections, to enable efficient collaborations among nearby edge servers to alleviate the traffic between cloud and edge servers and improve the system performance with saved bandwidth cost and enhanced data rate.
- **Connection**: the data routing among edge servers needs to consider the features of connections among edge servers. Specifically, edge server can be connected with each other using the wired connections over Internet or wireless connections through opportunistic connections. For example, [21] proposes a vehicular edge computing system where contents are shipped among edge servers by opportunistic vehicular contacts.

1.3 Advantages of Edge Computing

The motivation of edge computing is to place the contents and application services as close to their consumers as possible. In particular, we argue that the edge computing is dedicated to serving mobile users by addressing the shortage of location-awareness of cloud computing.

Specifically, in contrast to traditional PC users, mobile users have predictable service demands subject to their locations [12]. For example, a mobile user in a shopping center tends to be interested in the local sales, open hour, restaurants, and events inside the attended shopping center; such information become rusty once he/she leaves the shopping center. In another example, a visitor to a new town would seek for the information on the places of interest, news, and weather conditions inside the town, while uninterested in similar information of other sites. For example, 90% of US smartphone owners use location-based applications to get directions, recommendations, or other information [22].

Cloud computing provides a central portal of information but lacks location-awareness. Such model is suitable for indoor PC users with a high-rate wired connection; it is however not only costly for mobile users using expensive cellular bandwidth but also inconvenient as mobile users have to punch fingers over a slim touch screen to dig in a global pool of information for specific localized contents. As an example shown in Fig. 1.4, assuming that a mobile user inside a shopping center is to access the localized store flyers within the shopping center. To do this using the cloud, the store owner has to first upload its flyers to a remote cloud server, and then direct mobile users to the cloud for content retrieval, although the store and mobile user are proximity to each other.

Edge computing overcomes this issue by providing engaged localized services subject to the specific deployment sites. In the same example in Fig. 1.5, an edge server can be installed inside the shopping center and pre-cache the flyers. The

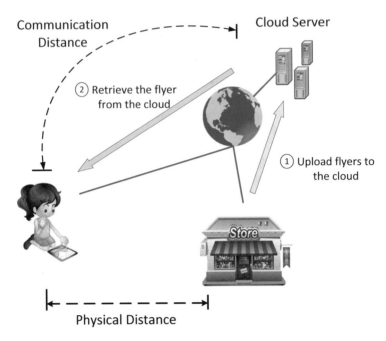

Fig. 1.4 Retrieving the flyer from the cloud

mobile users can therefore enjoy high-rate free local connections without the need to dig the information over cloud.

As indicated in this example, the edge computing brings two immediate advantages:

- **Enhanced service quality to mobile users**: As compared to cloud, edge computing can provide enhanced service quality with much increased data rate and reduced service latency and response time. Moreover, by downloading through local connections without going through the backbone network, the users can benefit from the reduced bandwidth cost.
- **Enhanced efficiency to network**: Edge computing avoids the back-and-forth traffic between cloud and mobile users. This not only saves the backbone bandwidth but also significantly reduces the energy consumption and carbon footprint of core networks, and it therefore represents a promising approach toward the sustainable development of networking [23].

Edge Computing vs Cloud Computing
With cloud computing becoming the overarching Internet approach for information storage, retrieval, and management, and mobile devices becoming the major outlets of service applications, the successful integration of cloud computing and mobile

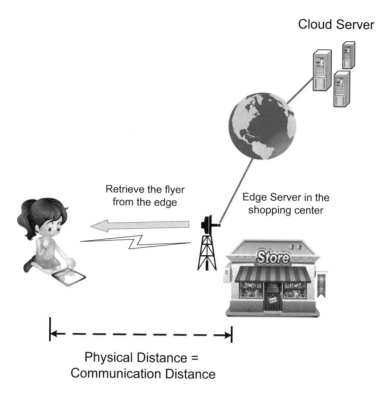

Fig. 1.5 Retrieving the flyer from the edge

devices therefore represents the key task for the next generation network. This however faces several fundamental challenges:

- **Agility of services**: Unlike PC users which typically ask for traditional Internet applications, such as emails and Internet surfing, mobile users wearing mobile devices on the go may request diverse applications, e.g., ehealthcare, Internet-of-Things (IoT) applications, which adapt to their locations and environments. The centralized cloud can hardly manage the diverse service requests from dynamic mobile users.
- **Real-time response**: With mobile devices limited in resources by nature, mobile applications typically need to outsource their computation jobs to the cloud and expect real-time response. The emerging wearable devices, e.g., Google glasses and Microsoft Hololens, would rely even more intensively on cloud to support their real-time sensing and data processing applications.
- **Long-thin connection**: The enjoyable high-rate data exchange between cloud and mobile is fundamental to support the resource-hungry mobile applications. This, however, is still impractical which is impeded by the long-thin connections between mobile users and remote cloud. The high wireless bandwidth cost is

also daunting to mobile users. As reported by a recent Cisco survey, even of poor reliability and security, WiFi is still favored by 50% of smartphone users and over 80% tablets, laptop, and eReader users than cellular networks due to its low cost.

To overcome the above issues between cloud and mobile applications, edge computing has recently emerged as a more practical solution to enable the smooth convergence between cloud and mobile for content delivery and real-time data processing. The major difference between cloud computing and edge computing is on the support of location-awareness. The cloud computing locates in a centralized place and serves as a centralized global portal of information; cloud computing often lacks location-awareness. The edge computing extends cloud to reside at user's premises and dedicates on localized service applications. Table 1.1 summarizes the differences between edge computing and cloud computing.

Note that the edge servers at different locations can be deployed by separate operators and owners and form a collaborative edge computing system in the wide region. For example, [21] describes a distributed vehicular edge computing system where edge servers in a city are deployed by separate entities for their own commercial usage. The edge servers deployed by different owners work in a fully distributed manner and are formed as an integrated content distribution network for disseminating media contents to vehicles across the city. In the example of [21], the content files to distribute are uploaded to the edge servers by their owners using local wireless connections.

1.4   Exemplary Applications

Edge computing, composed of geo-distributed edge servers, targets to deliver the localized and location-based services. In what follows, we showcase some examples of edge computing implementation from this perspective. Some other use cases of edge computing in IoT applications are described in [24, 25].

- **Shopping Center**
  A number of edge servers can be deployed at different levels of a multi-floor shopping center and collectively form an integrated localized edge computing information system. The edge servers at different levels can pre-cache floor-specific contents, such as the layout and ads of stores on the current floor, and provide accurate location-based applications including indoor navigation, ads distribution, and feedback collections to mobile users through WiFi.
- **Park**
  The edge computing system can be deployed in a park to provide localized tourism services. For instance, edge servers can be deployed at the entrance or important locations inside the park. The edge server at the park entrance can pre-cache information including map and tourist guide; other edge servers at different locations inside the park can be incorporated with sensor networks for environment monitoring and provide navigation and alert information to tourists.

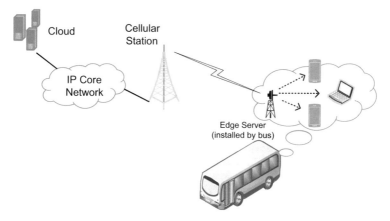

Fig. 1.6 On-board Edge computing system

- **Inter-state Bus**
  Greyhound has launched "BLUE" [10], an on-board edge computing system over inter-state buses for entertainment services. As an example illustrated in Fig. 1.6, an edge server can be deployed inside the bus and provides on-board video streaming, gaming, and social networking services to passengers using WiFi. The on-board edge server connects to the cloud through cellular networks to update the pre-cached contents. Using its computing facility, the edge server can also collect and process the utility data of users, such as number of passengers on-board and their access behaviors, and report to cloud.

References

1. N. Ahmed, D. De, I. Hussain, Internet of things (IoT) for smart precision agriculture and farming in rural areas. IEEE Internet of Things J. **5**(6), 4890–4899 (2018)
2. M. Satyanarayanan, The emergence of edge computing. Computer **50**(1), 30–39 (2017)
3. N. Hautiere, J. Tarel, D. Aubert, Towards fog-free in-vehicle vision systems through contrast restoration, in *2007 IEEE Conference on Computer Vision and Pattern Recognition* (2007), pp. 1–8
4. Y. Qu, S. Yu, W. Zhou, Y. Tian, GAN-driven personalized spatial-temporal private data sharing in cyber-physical social systems. IEEE Trans. Netw. Sci. Eng. **7**(4), 2576–2586 (2020)
5. X. Wang, Z. Ning, L. Wang, Offloading in internet of vehicles: a fog-enabled real-time traffic management system. IEEE Trans. Ind. Inf. **14**(10), 4568–4578 (2018)
6. X. Hou, Y. Li, M. Chen, D. Wu, D. Jin, S. Chen, Vehicular fog computing: a viewpoint of vehicles as the infrastructures. IEEE Trans. Veh. Technol. **65**(6), 3860–3873 (2016)
7. N. Abbas, Y. Zhang, A. Taherkordi, T. Skeie, Mobile edge computing: a survey. IEEE Internet of Things J. **5**(1), 450–465 (2018)
8. F. Jalali, K. Hinton, R. Ayre, T. Alpcan, R.S. Tucker, Fog computing may help to save energy in cloud computing. IEEE J. Select. Areas Commun. **34**(5), 1728–1739 (2016)

9. L. Gu, D. Zeng, S. Guo, A. Barnawi, Y. Xiang, Cost efficient resource management in fog computing supported medical cyber-physical system. IEEE Trans. Emerg. Top. Comput. **5**(1), 108–119 (2017)
10. Greyhound Media Relations, Greyhound Launches "BLUE", an Exclusive Wi-Fi Enabled Onboard Entertainment System. https://www.greyhound.com/en/newsroom/viewrelease.aspx? id=528&year=2013. Accessed Dec 2014
11. F. Bonomi, R. Milito, J. Zhu, S. Addepalli, Fog computing and its role in the Internet of Things, in *Proceedings of ACM MCC* (2012), pp. 13–16
12. E. Baştuğ, M. Bennis, M. Debbah, Living on the edge: the role of proactive caching in 5G wireless networks. IEEE Commun. Mag. **52**, 82–89 (2014)
13. G. Peng, CDN: Content Distribution Network (2004). arXiv. Preprint cs/0411069
14. B. Ahlgren, C. Dannewitz, C. Imbrenda, D. Kutscher, B. Ohlman, A survey of information-centric networking. IEEE Commun. Mag. **50**(7), 26–36 (2012)
15. S.R. Pokhrel, Y. Qu, S. Nepal, S. Singh, Privacy-aware autonomous valet parking: towards experience driven approach. IEEE Trans. Intell. Transport. Syst. **PP**, 1–12 (2020)
16. M. Satyanarayanan, Z. Chen, K. Ha, W. Hu, W. Richter, P. Pillai, Cloudlets: at the Leading Edge of Mobile-Cloud Convergence, in *Proceedings of MobiCASE* (2014)
17. Y. Zhang, Y. Zhou, Transparent computing: a new paradigm for pervasive computing, in *Ubiquitous Intelligence and Computing* (2006), pp. 1–11
18. M. Satyanarayanan, P. Bahl, R. Caceres, N. Davies, The case for VM-based cloudlets in mobile computing. IEEE Pervas. Comput. **8**(4), 14–23 (2009)
19. C. Meurisch, A. Seeliger, B. Schmidt, I. Schweizer, F. Kaup, M. Mühlhäuser, Upgrading wireless home routers for enabling large-scale deployment of cloudlets, in *Mobile Computing, Applications, and Services* (Springer, New York, 2015), pp. 12–29
20. D. Kreutz, F.M.V. Ramos, P.E. Verissimo, C.E. Rothenberg, S. Azodolmolky, S. Uhlig, Software-defined networking: a comprehensive survey. Proc. IEEE **103**(1), 14–76 (2015)
21. T.H. Luan, L.X. Cai, J. Chen, X. Shen, F. Bai, VTube: towards the media rich city life with autonomous vehicular content distribution, in *Proceedings of IEEE SECON* (2011), pp. 359–367
22. eMarketer, Most Smartphone Owners Use Location-Based Services. https://www.emarketer.com/Article/Most-Smartphone-Owners-Use-Location-Based-Services/1013863. Accessed April 2017
23. X. Zhang, Z. Xu, L. Fan, S. Yu, Y. Qu, Near-optimal energy-efficient algorithm for virtual network function placement. IEEE Trans. Cloud Comput. **PP**(99), 1-1 (2019)
24. Cisco White Paper, Cisco fog computing solutions: unleash the power of the Internet of Things (2015)
25. I. Stojmenovic, S. Wen, X. Huang, T.H. Luan, An overview of fog computing and its security issues. Concurr. Comput. Pract. Exp. **28**(10), 2991–3005 (2015)

Chapter 2
Privacy Issues in Edge Computing

Edge computing extends computing from the cloud to the end near the user and directly processes and makes decisions on the data locally [1]. To a certain extent, it avoids the long-distance transmission of data in the network and reduces the risk of privacy disclosure [2]. However, because edge devices obtain first-hand user data, they can obtain sensitive privacy data. For example, in the edge computing scenario of telecom operators, curious users of edge nodes can easily collect and pry into other users' location information, service content, and usage frequency. In most of edge computing scenarios, edge nodes lack effective encryption or desensitization measures compared with traditional cloud centers [3]. Once attacked, sniffed, and corroded by hackers, stored household consumption, personal health information in the electronic medical system, road event vehicle information, etc. will be leaked.

Due to real-time data processing, heterogeneous data sources, limited resources from end devices, and the complexity of access devices [4], the security and privacy mechanism of the traditional cloud computing environment are no longer suitable for protecting massive data generated by the edge computing paradigm. The privacy problems of location-aware data, context-aware data, and protection level performance are challenges that the edge computing paradigm must address [5].

The user data in edge computing are usually stored and processed in authorized entities, such as edge data centers and infrastructure providers [6]. The types of data include user identity information, location information, and sensitive data. However, these authorized entities are semi-trusted because users' privacy information has the risk of being attacked by adversaries. Furthermore, in the open ecosystem of edge computing, multiple trust domains are controlled by different infrastructure providers. In this case, it is impossible for users to know in advance whether a service provider is trustworthy [7]. Therefore, there is a high possibility of data leakage or loss that endangers user privacy.

© The Author(s), under exclusive license to Springer Nature Singapore Pte Ltd. 2021
L. Gao et al., *Privacy-Preserving in Edge Computing*, Wireless Networks,
https://doi.org/10.1007/978-981-16-2199-4_2

This chapter summarizes the key privacy challenges in edge computing and their state of the art. We will propose our corresponding solutions in the following three chapters.

2.1   Context-Aware Privacy Issue

The purpose of edge computing is to concentrate data processing and applications in closer devices at the edge of network instead of processing all data in the cloud to reduce the heavy burden for the cloud and improve the computational time [8]. Edge computing is more hierarchical and has several layers that form the network, whereas edge computing relies on individual nodes that do not constitute the network [9]. Edge computing has a wide range of peer-to-peer interconnections among the nodes [10]. More accurately, the components of the edge and core networks, such as core routers, regional servers, and WAN switches, can be used as the edge computing infrastructure [11]. Moreover, the sensitive message density of IoTs devices and sensors is very high, which requires real-time privacy preservation for the requested service; thus, it is necessary to store and process the data of the IoTs in the vicinity of the IoTs transmission devices and sensors [12]. Service privacy should be minimally preserved for real-time IoTs applications.

In the edge computing environment, user privacy data are stored and processed by entities that are not under the control of users. Therefore, it is the current research focus to allow users to perform various operations, such as auditing, searching, and updating, on context-aware data while ensuring that the privacy of users is not attacked. Differential privacy has been widely utilized to develop an appreciated privacy-preserving model in edge computing [13],

Wang et al. [14] presented a differential privacy-based privacy-preserving scheme named Privacy-Preserving Content-Based Publish (PCP) that mainly focuses on content-based publishing and subscribing. The model first utilized the U-Apriori algorithm to measure the top-K frequent item sets, such as attributes from datasets, and applied the Laplace mechanism to ensure differential privacy.

A Ciphertext Policy-Attribute Based Encryption (CP-ABE) scheme for outsourcing cloud data privacy protection of mobile devices proposed by J. Maseedu et al. [15], which uses probabilistic public-key encryption and ranked keyword searching algorithms to achieve ranking queries of privacy protection on mobile terminals with limited resources [16]. First, mobile users generate a file index and encrypt and upload data and index [17]. In addition, to access the cipher-text data stored in the cloud, the user generates a trap door for the keyword and sends it to the cloud [18]. Furthermore, according to the search trapdoor, the cloud server returns the sorted matching data based on the correlation score to the user and then decrypts the original data.

Regarding the privacy-preserving approach in edge computing, a few papers have considered privacy issues in the single linkage between an edge node and the user [19]. Approaches include differential privacy [20], k-anonymity-based privacy preservation, t-closeness, and other variants. In addition, the PPFA model, which was described by Lyu [21], has been discussed for the use of differential privacy to innovate with homomorphic encryption to preserve the sensitive content during communication among multiple smart meters (edge nodes) and users [21]. Although these technologies provide good performance results, the results are more focused on a stable network instead of long-term dynamic or customizable network constraints [22].

Alsheikh [23] conducted deep research on the Markov Decision Process (MDP). In addition, the MDP scheme in privacy preservation has been successfully proven by Qu [24] and Wei [25] to have high effectiveness in social networks and context-aware applications on mobile phones. These methods have a solid theoretical foundation and provide high-level privacy protection in the edge computing environment.

In addition, customizable privacy protection is particularly difficult when context information is included. With the continuous growth in data, end users keep uploading newly generated data to the connected edge node. In this case, the upper-layer edge nodes continuously collect data and thereby analyze it with various big data techniques such as data mining [26]. As we cannot assume that all the edge nodes could be trusted, privacy disclosure is inevitable when the context is leveraged by adversaries in crossover analysis [27, 28]. Some current data privacy-preserving algorithms and methods are promoted in edge computing environments, such as k-anonymity [29], t-closeness [30], differential privacy [21], and homomorphic encryption [31]. However, the identified issues are barely discussed and cannot be individually solved by the above existing countermeasures.

All of the aforementioned problems pose a great challenge to achieve an optimal tradeoff between privacy protection and data utilities. In addition to privacy protection, data utility is equally important because it represents the overall system availability. We have observed that current service providers usually fail to provide long-term multistage privacy protection. Therefore, users may publish data anonymously or provide fake information to avoid privacy disclosure, which causes low data utility and thereby degrades the quality of service (QoS) of the system [32]. Distrust will propagate and finally cause the collapse of the hierarchical edge-driven structures.

2.2 Location-Aware Privacy Issue

As a significant technology of the IoTs, edge computing has a wide range of application environments [33], such as environmental monitoring, disaster early warning, traffic management, health care, industrial manufacturing, emergency rescue, and many other fields, helping people obtain a large number of accurate and reliable information at any time, any place, and any environmental conditions [34]. In the practical application process of edge computing, the wireless and distributed characteristics of edge nodes are vulnerable to adversaries, which leads to critical location-aware privacy disclosure problems [35]. For example, in the field of animal monitoring, adversaries can find and capture the location of rare animals by monitoring wireless edge nodes; in the field of intelligent transportation, adversaries can infer users' privacy information, such as life rules and behavior habits, through mobile trajectory data in edge nodes [36]. The location privacy disclosure problem exposed in edge computing seriously affects the application development of edge computing. It is of great significance to study location-aware privacy protection technology for the large-scale application of the edge computing paradigm.

With the popularity of location-based services, location privacy has become a research focus. At present, the research focus in this field is mainly focused on the use of k-anonymity and t-closeness techniques to achieve privacy protection in location services [37], but the k-anonymity-based location privacy protection scheme consumes considerable network bandwidth and computing costs in practical applications, which is not suitable for edge devices with limited resources.

Edge computing brings data closer to the user instead of relying on communication with the data center [11]. One of the key benefits of edge computing is the dense geographical distribution that can be achieved by deploying edge nodes in different locations and connecting each of these nodes to end devices [38]. This geographical distribution enables more efficient communication between end users or devices and the server [9]. The geographical distribution of the edge nodes also enables location-based mobility support for IoTs devices such that traversal of the entire network is not necessary [19]. This is distinct from the situation in a cloud network in which all data must be uploaded to the cloud side for computation, and data packets must then be sent back to the end devices [10]. This delays the communication of data, especially in environments with real-time application requirements such as for the control of oil pump valves. Apart from all the beneficial location-aware features from edge computing, the leading problem appears, the protection of users' location privacy.

Users in the edge computing paradigm are not expected to disclose their location information to adversary while receiving service [39]. In edge computing, the location-aware data include not only the current specific location but also the contents that are stored and processed within the edge node, such as moving track and behavior habits [40]. One of the most commonly used location-aware privacy-preserving solutions is spatial cloaking [41] in which the user disguises the location as a region and then sends it to the edge nodes. The edge nodes provide services for the user according to the location information when the user is connected to the network. In this way, the edge node cannot accurately know the location of the user. In fact, the intensity of location-aware privacy protection and the quality of service (QoS) is a pair of contradictory relations. Users are required to choose according to the specific situation. The existing research on location-aware privacy protection technology in edge computing is mainly carried out from two directions: the privacy-preserving method relying on trusted third-party institutions and the method based on network k-anonymity [12, 19].

In addition, the privacy-preserved pseudonym scheme proposed by J. Kang [42] discussed privacy issues in location-based edge computing Internet vehicles. Although these technologies provide good performance results, they are more focused on a stabilized network condition instead of dynamic and customized edge computing constraints.

For location-aware sensitive data, Software-Defined Network (SDN) provides real-time information about flexible and reliable available resources from both software and management perspectives [43, 44]. Centralized controllers enable optimal decision-making in location data privacy for each edge node. Moreover, dedicated control channels from SDN will enable high-level policies to be translated into low-level configuration instructions in order to support fine-grained control of location privacy data [43, 45]. Using SDN institutions to combine edge computing within a single network is designed to provide end users with a securer environment, as well as better resource pooling and agile network management [46].

SDN has been proven and widely applied to edge computing infrastructure [47–49]. SDN is designed to solve the challenges within edge computing by decoupling data and the control plane. The integration between SDN and edge computing can effectively improve the data utilities in terms of location privacy of the IoTs. Although the deployment of SDN with edge computing seems promising, privacy issues cannot be avoided [50].

Lyu et al. [21] conducted research on the customized ϵ-differential privacy-preserving methodology and it had successfully been proved by Qu et al. [24], Badsha et al. [51] and Wang et al. [25]. These approaches have high effectiveness in social networks, recommender systems, and location-aware applications [52]. They have solid theoretical foundations as well as provide high-level privacy protections [14].

In the progress of location-aware privacy preserving, adversaries can easily launch effective attacks by mining and utilizing background knowledge. Existing schemes lack adequate consideration for the background knowledge of time, user movement, and behavior models that adversaries might collect. Moreover, many schemes improves privacy payoff at the expense of service quality. Therefore, as a strict and provable metric, the methods such as ϵ-customizable differential privacy can obtain optimal tradeoff with high accuracy and efficiency. Furthermore, the methods of game theory such as multistage zero-sum game and Nash equilibrium can better solve the problem of interest balance between two or more parties.

2.3 Decentralized Privacy Issue

In edge computing, the environment is open to access, which poses great challenges from the perspective of privacy protection in real-world applications [53]. Hu et al. [54] devised a novel identity-based scheme to solve device-to-device and device-to-server communications in edge computing. However, there are potential risks due to the storage of the system's master key in every end device [55]. In addition, the scalability and resultant communication overhead are not taken into consideration. Privacy protection attracts increasing volume of interest from both academia and industry [56, 57]. From the perspective of anonymity, Kang et al. [58] designed a hybrid model that enhances the privacy protection by means of pseudonyms. Employing self-certification, it is possible to manage without the compromise of the system's robustness.

To further improve, Tan et al. [59] developed an end device identity authentication protocol of end devices and edge servers without certification, while Wazid et al. [60] proposed another secure authentication and key management scheme to improve key security of the users in IoTs scenarios [61]. In [62], Gu et al. proposed a customizable privacy protection model to enable the personalized privacy-preserving data sharing using Markov decision process [63]. This enables the private data sharing between end devices and edge servers, which meets numerous privacy demands. Nevertheless, these three models require a trusted third party, which is another bottleneck in terms of decentralized privacy protection [64].

Federated learning is a potential promising tool, which is proposed as a decentralized learning scheme where local data is distributed to the data owner [65, 66]. Federated learning enables each data owner to have a series of local learning parameters from the local model [67]. Rather than simply sharing the training data, the data owners share their local parameter updates with a trusted third party. Konecny et al. [68] explored the applicability of several current models and thereby devised an extension to address the sparse data issues. In [69], Konecny et al. further present a variant of federated learning which minimizes the communication cost by uploading a lessened number of local parameters. Smith et al. [66] devised a distributed learning model in terms of multiple relevant tasks using federated learning. Nishio et al. [70] also gave insights on how to select clients in a resource-limited mobile edge computing scenario. Lu et al. integrated federated learning into the consensus algorithm of blockchain to save the hashrate [71, 72]. Samarakoon et al. [73] devised a learning based intrusion detection based on sample selected extreme learning in edge computing. However, this work did not take sharing resources and device-to-device communication into consideration.

Blockchain has a specially designed distributed ledger structure that connects blocks in chronological order. The saved data is shared and maintained by all nodes in a decentralized environment. The leading advantages of blockchain are decentralization, non-tempering, open autonomy, and anonymous traceability [74]. By using blockchain, Jiao et al. [75] proposed a novel scheme to manage resource allocation for edge or cloud computing. Then, Rowan et al. [76] designed a blockchain-enhanced PKI with an inter-end device session key establishment protocol to provide privacy protection to device-to-device communications. Peng et al. [77] presented an on-board network anonymous authentication protocol. The strength of this model is guaranteeing the anonymity of users and efficient authentication, but it fails to detect malicious end devices. In addition, Lu et al. proposed a blockchain based reputation system and Malik proposed a blockchain based authentication in [78] and [79], respectively. Despite the characteristic of privacy preservation, these two models are incapable of end device announcement, which results in low scalability. To address the limitation of pre-storing lots of anonymous certificates, Lu et al. [80] designed a novel model to achieve conditional privacy. This model requires frequent change of anonymous certificates to avoid linkage attack, which hinders the performance of edge computing in terms of efficiency. In [81], blockchain meets distribute hash table (DHT), which decouples validation from state storage. To the best of our knowledge, no existing work has studied the joint use of blockchain and federated learning in the context of efficiently privacy-preserving communication in edge computing scenario.

2.4 Common Privacy Attacks and Potential Attacking Windows

With the deep integrations of Industrial Internet of Things (IIoTs), large number of IoTs sensing devices are deployed in the field of critical infrastructure to form edge computing model. Through the application of large-scale sensing devices and the decompression of cloud computing capacity, edge computing network has greatly extended computing services such as information acquisition and real-time control. Moreover, edge computing provides important application and functional support for the friendly interaction of users and the local interconnection monitoring services. However, the privacy problems will be more prominent under the requirement of real-time and high availability of edge computing. This section will conduct an in-depth analysis of the privacy challenges faced by edge networks. According to the architecture of edge computing network, the network security challenges it faces mainly focus on terminal, data, network, and system risks.

- **Malicious Terminal Penetration Attack:** The terminal domain of edge computing supports the interconnection of users and things, as well as things and things [82]. A large number of real-time control equipment, condition monitoring equipment, information collection equipment, and user equipment are widely used, and the network will have tens of thousands or even millions of sensing device nodes. Many kinds of IoTs sensing devices converge and are accessed by edge computing terminals, which are heterogeneous, diverse, and dynamic, so it is difficult to carry out distributed authorization authentication and behavior control [83]. Therefore, the access of malicious sensing devices improves the penetration attack risk of sensing device nodes taking the edge computing terminal as the springboard. Additionally, as traditional network devices, the firmware and system of edge computing terminals also have some vulnerabilities that are difficult to discover [84]. Once these vulnerabilities are exploited by hackers, they may have very serious consequences. In addition, when the edge computing terminal is deployed in the uncontrollable edge environment, it is easy for attackers to counterfeit and forge the edge computing terminal to carry out network penetration attacks on the edge network, resulting in network and information security events such as data leakage and system paralysis [85].

- **Sensitive Data Stealing and Tampering:** In the data domain of edge computing, the core purpose is to realize real-time interaction with the master control system after big data preprocessing at the user side and production site side to reduce the centralized computing pressure of the master station system and cloud computing center [86]. However, in the process of data exchange and sharing of the edge computing network, the attacker can eavesdrop, infiltrate, side-channel attack, tamper, and perform other destructive actions through new network attacks, which can lead to leaking user privacy, use information and passwords, intercepting transmission information and control instructions, and hijacking industrial control systems or edge computing terminals, which puts the entire system into a chaotic state [87]. Additionally, because the new network attack has changed from the traditional single point attack to a multipoint breakthrough, it is more difficult to detect and defend. However, the monitoring and control data transmitted by the edge computing network are based on a certain control period, which requires the continuity and real-time of the service, and these data require high real-time, certainty and stability [88]. Therefore, under the constraints of the uncertainty of attack characteristics and strong coupling of terminal—network—service, the highly reliable interaction is of great significance to attack active defense technology.
- **Ubiquitous Invasion:** In the transmission domain of edge computing, there are many types of networks that are widely distributed. Wireless mesh networks, ZigBee, 4G/5G, and other wireless networks are widely used for interconnection and interworking [89]. Therefore, transmission networks have become one of the important sources of risk to penetrate and attack edge computing networks. On the one hand, the network intrusion attack aiming at delaying, obstructing, or destroying the service ability of the edge computing terminal node, network, and system will cause the edge computing network to be out of control, the communication service to collapse, the system service to be paralyzed, and the high real-time and high continuity requirements of the edge computing service to be endangered [90]. On the other hand, the continuous evolution of new network attacks, traditional intrusion detection, and post defense security measures based on feature matching cannot deal with known attacks, so it is urgent to carry out research on active detection and defense technology for edge computing networks [91].
- **Attack Transmission of All Time Domain and Interconnection Services:** In the edge computing system domain, with the decrease in computing capabilities, the service system decreases to the edge side of the site with a wide area distribution and forms a new mode of full-time domain spatial interconnection with the cloud service of the main station [92]. Once a local network security attack occurs, it will spread rapidly in the network and then affect as many as millions or even more IoTs sensing devices and users. If measures to deal with network attacks are ineffective and untimely, it will seriously threaten the accuracy, confidentiality, and integrity of business logic. Furthermore, it may endanger the orderly and healthy operation of the whole system [93]. In smart grid systems, for example, the coupling between the physical power

grid system and the information network system is increasingly enhanced so that the network security risk introduced by power edge computing will further transmit to the power grid body [94]. The enormous edge computing network has produced a large number of network security alarm events, which cannot meet the requirements of relying on human event handling [95]. In addition, the current advanced persistent apt attack has changed from a traditional single point attack to a multipoint breakthrough, which makes it more difficult to detect and defend, and it is more difficult to detect and handle apt attacks in the full-time domain and ubiquitous Internet environment of edge computing systems. Therefore, fast and effective security event correlation analysis and collaborative disposal become another problem to be solved in the security protection of edge computing.

Potential attack windows in the edge computing environment, including edge access (cloud-edge access, edge-end device access), edge servers (hardware, software, data), edge management (account, management/service interface, administrator), as shown in the following Fig. 2.1 and Table 2.1. It summarizes the attacks faced by edge computing and the most important security challenge. These security challenges are ranked from high to low based on the research on the concerns of industrial edge computing enterprises and IoTs edge computing enterprises.

On account of the above privacy concerns in edge computing, we further summarize the common attacks. They are background knowledge attack, collusion attack, linkage attack, structural attack, forgery attack, eavesdropping attack, and Sybil attack. There are also some other forms of attacks such as tracking attacks [96] and inference attacks [97, 98], but these attacks fall in the range of the seven illustrated attacks. In the following sections, we further demonstrate the resistance of each protection models against attacks (Table 2.2).

- **Background Knowledge Attack:** Background knowledge attack is one of the most popular attacks under privacy scenarios in edge computing, especially when edge computing infrastructure deals with large amount of the context and location information. The rationale behind its proliferation is that it can be combined with other types of attacks. Background knowledge of a specific entry is easy to obtain in edge computing [99]. Moreover, the background knowledge of adversaries is hard to model, measure, and predict, which makes it more difficult to be defeated.
- **Collusion Attack:** Collusion attack is another wide-spread attack method. Collusion attack is especially mortal in edge computing circumstances. The reason is that a specific user can have multiple contacts in different edge nodes and therefore there might be multiple adversaries hiding in the contact list. As different adversary holds different background knowledge of this user, they can share the information with each other to launch a collusion attack [100]. In addition, collusion attack can also be combined with other forms of attacks. Figure 2.2 is a snapshot of collusion attack. This is the attack where multiple adversaries involve and make joint effort to reveal more sensitive information than what they have possessed.
- **Linkage Attack:** Linkage attack is experiencing rapid expansion with rapidly increasing data volume and data sources. For example, adversaries can make

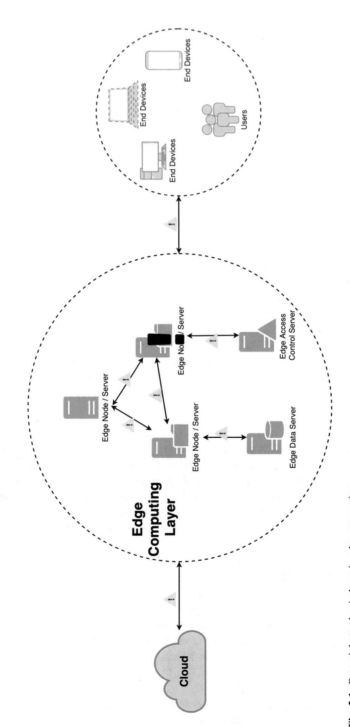

Fig. 2.1 Potential attack windows in edge computing

Table 2.1 Potential privacy attaching windows and challenges in edge computing

Attacking window	Potential privacy and security challenge
User—edge connection	Insecure communication protocols
	Malicious edge nodes
Edge nodes/servers	Insecure software systems and hardware components
	Initiate distributed denial of service (DoS)
	Spread advanced persistent threat (APT) attack
	Privacy preserving on user and edge nodes/servers data
	Security support on hardware
	Vulnerable to damage data in edge nodes/servers
Edge management	Insufficient identity, credentials, and access management
	Account information is vulnerable to be hijacked
	Insecure interfaces and APIs
	Malicious administrators

Table 2.2 Edge computing privacy issues and corresponding attacks

	Context-aware privacy	Location-aware privacy	Decentralized privacy
Background knowledge attack	Fully existed	Fully existed	Fully existed
Collusion attack	Fully existed	Fully existed	Fully existed
Linkage attack	Fully existed	Fully existed	Fully existed
Structural attack	Fully existed	Partially existed	Not supported
Forgery attack	Partially existed	Fully existed	Not supported
Eavesdropping attack	Fully existed	Fully existed	Fully existed
Sybil attack	Fully existed	Partially existed	Not supported

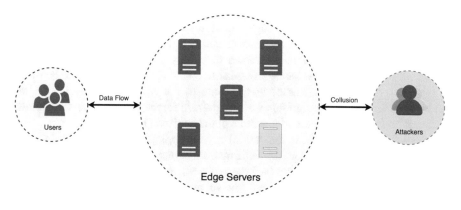

Fig. 2.2 Collusion attack snapshot

an attack based on multiple edge nodes and edge computing networks. Linkage attack has a good attack performance as adversaries can collect different category of data of the same user from multiple data sources [101]. Furthermore, machine learning based methods provide linkage attack better tools which help adversaries bypass the protection. Song et al. [102] developed a new type of inference attack. This type of the attack targets the sensitive context-aware browsing history of metadata band public click analytics through edge node connections. This attack only needs user profile information shortening services log, which are public and easy-to-access information once connection triggered. This can further reduce the attack overhead and upgrade accuracy by taking time-varying models of users into consideration.

- **Structural Attack:** Adversaries are proceeding to structural attacks because edge computing is usually modeled as a graph based on graph theory in both hardware and software mapping. In one hand, graph theory helps to better understand and establishes edge computing structure. On the other hand, adversaries can take advantage of the structural information to mount an attack. The most outstanding merit of structural attack is that adversaries can re-identify a specific user even without background knowledge. The structural attack is also widely deployed in de-anonymization. In [103], Chen et al. proposed two types of practical attacks to steal sensitive information from graph-based clustering methods. Targeted noise injection and small community are devised to attack three popular graph clustering models, including community discovery, node2vec, and singular value decomposition (SVD). Based on this, the authors found that adversaries with limited open-source background knowledge can launch successful attacks. In terms of simple defenses, it can decrease the success ratio to 25% by the cost of only 0.2% clusters over-noisy.

- **Forgery Attack:** In a forgery attack, misleading messages are generated with fake information, so that adversaries can initiate some other plotting attacks such as the location-tracking attack. There are five phases in a forgery attack, in which we use vehicular networks in edge computing as an example [104]. Firstly, the victim node and the adversary node establish a link with location information. Secondly, the adversary node creates malicious payload to the victim node. Thirdly, the victim node sends a request to social spot s_1 for cookies. Fourthly, s_1 gives the email address of victim node to the adversary node. Lastly, the certificates will be reset. In this way, an outside forgery attack is performed and the privacy of the victim nodes will be compromised [105].

- **Eavesdropping Attack:** In the case of eavesdropping attack, it is quite intuitive that adversaries eavesdrop the information communication and transmission process by means of modern hacking technologies, including Internet, electromagnetic wave, and so on. This type of attack is launched by unauthorized real-time interception of a private communication [106]. Therefore, it is vital

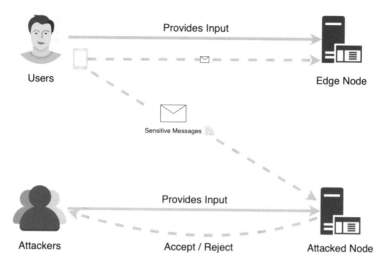

Fig. 2.3 Eavesdropping attack illustration

to secure communication to prevent privacy leakage. In Fig. 2.3, eavesdropping attack aims at stealing the sensitive information of users when the data during the transmission. It enables the attackers to breach the privacy without accessing the publicly shared data of the users.

- **Sybil Attack:** The Sybil attack is normally launched under the scenario of a reputation-involved edge computing system. During the attack process, an adversary generates a large number of pseudo names and further gains the maximum influence [107]. Based on the influence, the adversary can mislead the other users in the system or even fool the central authority. Privacy leakage happens during the attack. Whether the attack can be successfully launched is decided by the cost to fake identities and the trust mechanism between central authority and the identities. In [108], Liu et al. did a study on extended Sybil defenses. The authors found that current Sybil attack models in edge computing networks are static, which is not practical. This work takes temporal dynamics into consideration and involves three new features. Firstly, the new model considers the capabilities of adversaries to modify Sybil-controlled parts of a structural social graph. Secondly, it has the capabilities to modify the connections which Sybil identities of him/her maintain to honest users. Thirdly, the proposed model benefits from the regular dynamics of connections structure and thereby trains honest parts. In Fig. 2.4, adversaries in the scenario can quickly obtain the maximum influence in the network and launch relevant attacks to attack the sensitive data.

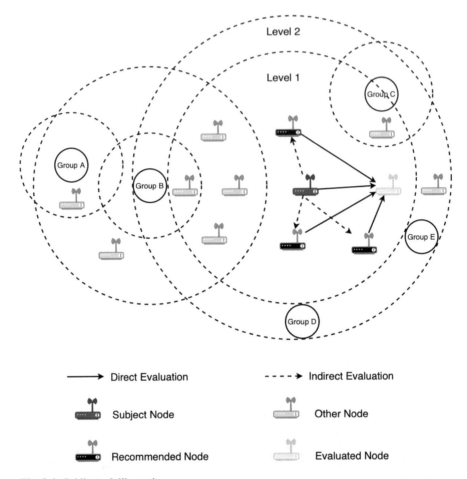

Fig. 2.4 Sybil attack illustration

References

1. M. Mukherjee, R. Matam, L. Shu, L. Maglaras, M.A. Ferrag, N. Choudhury, V. Kumar, Security and privacy in fog computing: challenges. IEEE Access **5**, 19293–19304 (2017)
2. J. Ni, A. Zhang, X. Lin, X.S. Shen, Security, privacy, and fairness in fog-based vehicular crowdsensing. IEEE Commun. Mag. **55**(6), 146–152 (2017)
3. K. Lee, D. Kim, D. Ha, U. Rajput, H. Oh, On security and privacy issues of fog computing supported internet of things environment, in *2015 6th International Conference on the Network of the Future (NOF)* (2015), pp. 1–3
4. R. Deng, R. Lu, C. Lai, T.H. Luan, H. Liang, Optimal workload allocation in fog-cloud computing toward balanced delay and power consumption. IEEE Internet of Things J. **3**(6), 1171–1181 (2016)
5. J. Oueis, E.C. Strinati, S. Barbarossa, The fog balancing: load distribution for small cell cloud computing, in *2015 IEEE 81st Vehicular Technology Conference (VTC Spring)* (2015), pp. 1–6

6. A. Alrawais, A. Alhothaily, C. Hu, X. Xing, X. Cheng, An attribute-based encryption scheme to secure fog communications. IEEE Access **5**, 9131–9138 (2017)

7. D. Preuveneers, W. Joosen, Edge-based and privacy-preserving multi-modal monitoring of student engagement in online learning environments, in *2019 IEEE International Conference on Edge Computing (EDGE)* (2019), pp. 18–20

8. W. Shi, J. Cao, Q. Zhang, Y. Li, L. Xu, Edge computing: vision and challenges. IEEE Internet of Things J. **3**(5), 637–646 (2016)

9. B. Gu, X. Wang, Y. Qu, J. Jin, Y. Xiang, L. Gao, Location-aware privacy preserving scheme in SDN-enabled fog computing, in *Security and Privacy in Digital Economy*, ed. by S. Yu, P. Mueller, J. Qian (Springer, Singapore, 2020), pp. 176–190

10. T.H. Luan, L. Gao, Z. Li, Y. Xiang, L. Sun, Fog computing: focusing on mobile users at the edge (2015). CoRR abs/1502.01815

11. L. Gao, T.H. Luan, S. Yu, W. Zhou, B. Liu, Fogroute: DTN-based data dissemination model in fog computing. IEEE Internet of Things J. **4**(1), 225–235 (2017)

12. L. Ma, X. Liu, Q. Pei, Y. Xiang, Privacy-preserving reputation management for edge computing enhanced mobile crowdsensing. IEEE Trans. Serv. Comput. **12**(5), 1–1 (2018)

13. X. Zhang, Q. Chen, X. Peng, X. Jiang, Differential privacy-based indoor localization privacy protection in edge computing, in *2019 IEEE SmartWorld, Ubiquitous Intelligence Computing, Advanced Trusted Computing, Scalable Computing Communications, Cloud Big Data Computing, Internet of People and Smart City Innovation (SmartWorld/SCALCOM/UIC/ATC/CBDCom/IOP/SCI)* (2019), pp. 491–496

14. Q. Wang, D. Chen, N. Zhang, Z. Ding, Z. Qin, PCP: a privacy-preserving content-based publish–subscribe scheme with differential privacy in fog computing. IEEE Access **5**, 17962–17974 (2017)

15. J. Maseedu, S.K. Pasupuleti, Attribute based range search over encrypted data for privacy preserving in cloud computing, in *2018 International Conference on Advances in Computing, Communications and Informatics (ICACCI)* (2018), pp. 323–329

16. R. Xu, B. Palanisamy, J. Joshi, Queryguard: privacy-preserving latency-aware query optimization for edge computing, in *2018 17th IEEE International Conference on Trust, Security and Privacy in Computing and Communications/12th IEEE International Conference on Big Data Science and Engineering (TrustCom/BigDataSE)* (2018), pp. 1097–1106

17. X. Xu, B. Tang, G. Jiang, X. Liu, Y. Xue, Y. Yuan, Privacy-aware data offloading for mobile devices in edge computing, in *2019 International Conference on Internet of Things (iThings) and IEEE Green Computing and Communications (GreenCom) and IEEE Cyber, Physical and Social Computing (CPSCom) and IEEE Smart Data (SmartData)* (2019), pp. 170–175

18. D. Yuan, X. Zhu, Y. Mao, B. Zheng, T. Wu, Privacy-preserving pedestrian detection for smart city with edge computing, in *2019 11th International Conference on Wireless Communications and Signal Processing (WCSP)* (2019), pp. 1–6

19. T. Wang, J. Zhou, X. Chen, G. Wang, A. Liu, Y. Liu, A three-layer privacy preserving cloud storage scheme based on computational intelligence in fog computing. IEEE Trans. Emerg. Top. Comput. Intell. **2**(1), 3–12 (2018)

20. C. Dwork, Differential privacy: a survey of results, in *Theory and Applications of Models of Computation*, ed. by M. Agrawal, D. Du, Z. Duan, A. Li (Springer, Berlin, Heidelberg, 2008), pp. 1–19

21. L. Lyu, K. Nandakumar, B. Rubinstein, J. Jin, J. Bedo, M. Palaniswami, PPFA: privacy preserving fog-enabled aggregation in smart grid. IEEE Trans. Ind. Inf. **14**(8), 3733–3744 (2018)

22. Y. Qu, S. Yu, W. Zhou, S. Chen, J. Wu, Customizable reliable privacy-preserving data sharing in cyber-physical social network. IEEE Trans. Netw. Sci. Eng. **8**(1), 269–281 (2020)

23. M. Abu Alsheikh, D.T. Hoang, D. Niyato, H. Tan, S. Lin, Markov decision processes with applications in wireless sensor networks: a survey. IEEE Commun. Surv. Tutor. **17**(3), 1239–1267 (thirdquarter 2015)

24. Y. Qu, S. Yu, L. Gao, W. Zhou, S. Peng, A hybrid privacy protection scheme in cyber-physical social networks. IEEE Trans. Comput. Soc. Syst. **5**(3), 773–784 (2018)

25. W. Wang, Q. Zhang, Privacy preservation for context sensing on smartphone. IEEE/ACM Trans. Network. **24**(6), 3235–3247 (2016)
26. Z. Wang, J. Hu, R. Lv, J. Wei, Q. Wang, D. Yang, H. Qi, Personalized privacy-preserving task allocation for mobile crowdsensing. IEEE Trans. Mob. Comput. **18**(6), 1330–1341 (2019)
27. Z. Wang, X. Pang, Y. Chen, H. Shao, Q. Wang, L. Wu, H. Chen, H. Qi, Privacy-preserving crowd-sourced statistical data publishing with an untrusted server. IEEE Trans. Mob. Comput. **18**(6), 1356–1367 (2019)
28. Y. Qu, M.R. Nosouhi, L. Cui, S. Yu, Privacy preservation in smart cities, in *Smart Cities Cybersecurity and Privacy*, Chapter 6, ed. by D.B. Rawat, K.Z. Ghafoor (Elsevier, Amsterdam, 2019), pp. 75–88
29. S. Vijayarani, A. Tamilarasi, M. Sampoorna, Analysis of privacy preserving k-anonymity methods and techniques, in *2010 International Conference on Communication and Computational Intelligence (INCOCCI)*, December 2010, pp. 540–545
30. N. Li, T. Li, S. Venkatasubramanian, t-Closeness: privacy beyond k-anonymity and l-diversity, in *2007 IEEE 23rd International Conference on Data Engineering*, April 2007, pp. 106–115
31. Y. Wang, T. Uehara, R. Sasaki, Fog computing: issues and challenges in security and forensics, in *2015 IEEE 39th Annual Computer Software and Applications Conference*, July 2015, vol. 3, pp. 53–59
32. S.R. Pokhrel, Y. Qu, L. Gao, QoS-aware personalized privacy with multipath TCP for industrial IoT: analysis and design. IEEE Internet of Things J. **7**(6), 4849–4861 (2020)
33. S. Yi, Z. Hao, Z. Qin, Q. Li, Fog computing: platform and applications, in *2015 Third IEEE Workshop on Hot Topics in Web Systems and Technologies (HotWeb)*, November 2015, pp. 73–78
34. M. Peng, S. Yan, K. Zhang, C. Wang, Fog-computing-based radio access networks: issues and challenges. IEEE Netw. **30**(4), 46–53 (2016)
35. R. Lu, K. Heung, A.H. Lashkari, A.A. Ghorbani, A lightweight privacy-preserving data aggregation scheme for fog computing-enhanced IoT. IEEE Access **5**, 3302–3312 (2017)
36. T.N. Gia, M. Jiang, A. Rahmani, T. Westerlund, P. Liljeberg, H. Tenhunen, Fog computing in healthcare internet of things: a case study on ECG feature extraction, in *2015 IEEE International Conference on Computer and Information Technology; Ubiquitous Computing and Communications; Dependable, Autonomic and Secure Computing; Pervasive Intelligence and Computing* (2015), pp. 356–363
37. I. Natgunanathan, A. Mehmood, Y. Xiang, L. Gao, S. Yu, Location privacy protection in smart health care system. IEEE Internet of Things J. **6**(2), 3055–3069 (2019)
38. I. Stojmenovic, S. Wen, The fog computing paradigm: scenarios and security issues, in *2014 Federated Conference on Computer Science and Information Systems*, September 2014, pp. 1–8
39. Y. Qu, J. Zhang, R. Li, X. Zhang, X. Zhai, S. Yu, Generative adversarial networks enhanced location privacy in 5G networks. Sci. China Inf. Sci. **63**(12), 1–12 (2020)
40. X. Wang, B. Gu, Y. Qu, Y. Ren, Y. Xiang, L. Gao, Reliable customized privacy-preserving in fog computing, in *ICC 2020 - 2020 IEEE International Conference on Communications (ICC)* (2020), pp. 1–6
41. T. Wang, J. Zeng, M.Z.A. Bhuiyan, H. Tian, Y. Cai, Y. Chen, B. Zhong, Trajectory privacy preservation based on a fog structure for cloud location services. IEEE Access **5**, 7692–7701 (2017)
42. J. Kang, R. Yu, X. Huang, Y. Zhang, Privacy-preserved pseudonym scheme for fog computing supported internet of vehicles. IEEE Trans. Intell. Transport. Syst. **19**(8), 2627–2637 (2018)
43. D. Kreutz, F.M.V. Ramos, P.E. Verissimo, C.E. Rothenberg, S. Azodolmolky, S. Uhlig, Software-defined networking: a comprehensive survey. Proc. IEEE **103**(1), 14–76 (2015)
44. S. Sezer, S. Scott-Hayward, P.K. Chouhan, B. Fraser, D. Lake, J. Finnegan, N. Viljoen, M. Miller, N. Rao, Are we ready for SDN? Implementation challenges for software-defined networks. IEEE Commun. Mag. **51**(7), 36–43 (2013)

45. B.A.A. Nunes, M. Mendonca, X. Nguyen, K. Obraczka, T. Turletti, A survey of software-defined networking: past, present, and future of programmable networks. IEEE Commun. Surv. Tutor. **16**(3), 1617–1634 (2014)
46. A. Soua, S. Tohme, Multi-level SDN with vehicles as fog computing infrastructures: a new integrated architecture for 5G-VANETs, in *2018 21st Conference on Innovation in Clouds, Internet and Networks and Workshops (ICIN)* (2018), pp. 1–8
47. C. Li, Z. Qin, E. Novak, Q. Li, Securing SDN infrastructure of IoT fog networks from MitM attacks. IEEE Internet of Things J. **4**(5), 1156–1164 (2017)
48. A.J. Kadhim, S.A. Hosseini Seno, Maximizing the utilization of fog computing in internet of vehicle using SDN. IEEE Commun. Lett. **23**(1), 140–143 (2019)
49. N.B. Truong, G.M. Lee, Y. Ghamri-Doudane, Software defined networking-based vehicular adhoc network with fog computing, in *2015 IFIP/IEEE International Symposium on Integrated Network Management (IM)* (2015), pp. 1202–1207
50. A.C. Baktir, A. Ozgovde, C. Ersoy, How can edge computing benefit from software-defined networking: a survey, use cases, and future directions. IEEE Commun. Surv. Tutor. **19**(4), 2359–2391 (fourthquarter 2017)
51. S. Badsha, X. Yi, I. Khalil, D. Liu, S. Nepal, E. Bertino, K. Lam, Privacy preserving location-aware personalized web service recommendations. IEEE Trans. Serv. Comput. 1–1 (2018). https://doi.org/10.1109/TSC.2018.2839587
52. X. Wang, B. Gu, Y. Ren, W. Ye, S. Yu, Y. Xiang, L. Gao, A fog-based recommender system. IEEE Internet of Things J. **7**(2), 1048–1060 (2020)
53. J. Ni, K. Zhang, Y. Yu, X. Lin, X.S. Shen, Providing task allocation and secure deduplication for mobile crowdsensing via fog computing, in *IEEE Transactions on Dependable and Secure Computing* (2018)
54. P. Hu, H. Ning, T. Qiu, H. Song, Y. Wang, X. Yao, Security and privacy preservation scheme of face identification and resolution framework using fog computing in internet of things. IEEE Internet of Things J. **4**(5), 1143–1155 (2017)
55. D.X. Song, D.A. Wagner, A. Perrig, Practical techniques for searches on encrypted data, in *2000 IEEE Symposium on Security and Privacy*, Berkeley, CA, May 14–17 (2000), pp. 44–55
56. R. Lu, X. Lin, T.H. Luan, X. Liang, X. (Sherman) Shen, Pseudonym changing at social spots: an effective strategy for location privacy in VANETs. IEEE Trans. Veh. Technol. **61**(1), 86–96 (2012)
57. H. Li, D. Liu, Y. Dai, T.H. Luan, S. Yu, Personalized search over encrypted data with efficient and secure updates in mobile clouds. IEEE Trans. Emerg. Top. Comput. **6**(1), 97–109 (2018)
58. J. Kang, R. Yu, X. Huang, Y. Zhang, Privacy-preserved pseudonym scheme for fog computing supported internet of vehicles. IEEE Trans. Intell. Transport. Syst. **19**(8), 2627–2637 (2018)
59. H. Tan, D. Choi, P. Kim, S.B. Pan, I. Chung, Secure certificateless authentication and road message dissemination protocol in VANETs. Wirel. Commun. Mob. Comput. **2018**, 7978027:1–7978027:13 (2018)
60. M. Wazid, A.K. Das, V. Odelu, N. Kumar, M. Conti, M. Jo, Design of secure user authenticated key management protocol for generic IoT networks. IEEE Internet of Things J. **5**(1), 269–282 (2018)
61. B. Liu, W. Zhou, L. Gao, H. Zhou, T.H. Luan, S. Wen, Malware propagations in wireless ad hoc networks. IEEE Trans. Depend. Secure Comput. **15**(6), 1016–1026 (2018)
62. B.S. Gu, L. Gao, X. Wang, Y. Qu, J. Jin, S. Yu, Privacy on the edge: customizable privacy-preserving context sharing in hierarchical edge computing. IEEE Transactions on Network Science and Engineering, Privacy on the edge: customizable privacy-preserving context sharing in hierarchical edge computing. IEEE Trans. Netw. Sci. Eng. **2019**, 12 (2019)
63. L. Cui, Y. Qu, M.R. Nosouhi, S. Yu, J.-W. Niu, G. Xie, Improving data utility through game theory in personalized differential privacy. J. Comput. Sci. Technol. **34**(2), 272–286 (2019)
64. H. Li, R. Lu, J.V. Misic, M.M.E.A. Mahmoud, Security and privacy of connected vehicular cloud computing. IEEE Netw. **32**(3), 4–6 (2018)

65. X. Wang, Y. Han, C. Wang, Q. Zhao, X. Chen, M. Chen, In-edge AI: intelligentizing mobile edge computing, caching and communication by federated learning. IEEE Network **33**(5), 156–165 (2019)
66. V. Smith, C.-K. Chiang, M. Sanjabi, A.S. Talwalkar, Federated multi-task learning, in *Advances in Neural Information Processing Systems 30: Annual Conference on Neural Information Processing Systems 2017*, 4–9 December 2017, Long Beach, CA (2017), pp. 4424–4434
67. L. Ma, Q. Pei, L. Zhou, H. Zhu, L. Wang, Y. Ji, Federated data cleaning: collaborative and privacy-preserving data cleaning for edge intelligence. IEEE Internet of Things J. **8**(8), 6757–6770 (2020)
68. J. Konecný, H. Brendan McMahan, D. Ramage, P. Richtárik, Federated optimization: distributed machine learning for on-device intelligence (2016). CoRR abs/1610.02527
69. J. Konecný, H. Brendan McMahan, F.X. Yu, P. Richtárik, A.T. Suresh, D. Bacon, Federated learning: strategies for improving communication efficiency (2016). CoRR abs/1610.05492
70. T. Nishio, R. Yonetani, Client selection for federated learning with heterogeneous resources in mobile edge, in *2019 IEEE International Conference on Communications, ICC 2019*, Shanghai, May 20–24 (2019), pp. 1–7
71. Y. Lu, X. Huang, Y. Dai, S. Maharjan, Y. Zhang, Blockchain and federated learning for privacy-preserved data sharing in industrial IoT. IEEE Trans. Ind. Inf. **16**(6), 4177–4186 (2019)
72. Y. Qu, S.R. Pokhrel, S. Garg, L. Gao, Y. Xiang, A blockchained federated learning framework for cognitive computing in industry 4.0 networks. IEEE Trans. Ind. Inf. **17**(4), 2964–2973 (2020)
73. X. An, X. Zhou, X. Lü, F. Lin, L. Yang, Sample selected extreme learning machine based intrusion detection in fog computing and MEC. Wirel. Commun. Mob. Comput. **2018** (2018). https://doi.org/10.1155/2018/7472095
74. L. Ma, Q. Pei, Y. Qu, K. Fan, X. Lai, Decentralized privacy-preserving reputation management for mobile crowdsensing, in *International Conference on Security and Privacy in Communication Systems* (Springer, New York, 2019), pp. 532–548
75. Y. Jiao, P. Wang, D. Niyato, K. Suankaewmanee, Auction mechanisms in cloud/fog computing resource allocation for public blockchain networks. IEEE Trans. Parallel Distrib. Syst. **30**(9), 1975–1989 (2019)
76. S. Rowan, M. Clear, M. Gerla, M. Huggard, C. Mc Goldrick, Securing vehicle to vehicle communications using blockchain through visible light and acoustic side-channels (2017). CoRR abs/1704.02553
77. N. Ruan, M. Li, J. Li, A novel broadcast authentication protocol for internet of vehicles. Peer-to-Peer Network. Appl. **10**(6), 1331–1343 (2017)
78. Z. Lu, W. Liu, Q. Wang, G. Qu, Z. Liu, A privacy-preserving trust model based on blockchain for vanets. IEEE Access **6**, 45655–45664 (2018)
79. N. Malik, P. Nanda, A. Arora, X. He, D. Puthal, Blockchain based secured identity authentication and expeditious revocation framework for vehicular networks, in *17th IEEE International Conference on Trust, Security and Privacy in Computing and Communications/12th IEEE International Conference on Big Data Science and Engineering, TrustCom/BigDataSE 2018*, New York, NY, August 1–3 (2018), pp. 674–679
80. R. Lu, X. Lin, H. Zhu, P.-H. Ho, X. Shen, ECPP: efficient conditional privacy preservation protocol for secure vehicular communications, in *INFOCOM 2008. 27th IEEE International Conference on Computer Communications, Joint Conference of the IEEE Computer and Communications Societies*, 13–18 April 2008, Phoenix, AZ, pp. 1229–1237
81. M. Bernardini, D. Pennino, M. Pizzonia, Blockchains meet distributed hash tables: decoupling validation from state storage (2019). Preprint. arXiv: 1904.01935
82. Q. Li, S. Meng, S. Zhang, J. Hou, L. Qi, Complex attack linkage decision-making in edge computing networks. IEEE Access **7**, 12058–12072 (2019)

83. H. Zhang, Q. Li, Y. Qi, J. Hou, Y. Liu, The research reviewed of edge network active safety defense technology, in *2019 IEEE Fifth International Conference on Big Data Computing Service and Applications (BigDataService)* (2019), pp. 242–246

84. Y. Ding, Y. Shi, A. Wang, X. Zheng, Z. Wang, G. Zhang, Adaptive chosen-plaintext collision attack on masked aes in edge computing. IEEE Access **7**, 63217–63229 (2019)

85. M. Yahuza, M.Y.I.B. Idris, A.W.B.A. Wahab, A.T.S. Ho, S. Khan, S.N.B. Musa, A.Z.B. Taha, Systematic review on security and privacy requirements in edge computing: state of the art and future research opportunities. IEEE Access **8**, 76541–76567 (2020)

86. J. Chi, E. Owusu, X. Yin, T. Yu, W. Chan, Y. Liu, H. Liu, J. Chen, S. Sim, V. Iyengar, P. Tague, Y. Tian, Privacy partition: a privacy-preserving framework for deep neural networks in edge networks, in *2018 IEEE/ACM Symposium on Edge Computing (SEC)* (2018), pp. 378–380

87. Q. Xu, Z. Su, K. Zhang, P. Li, Intelligent cache pollution attacks detection for edge computing enabled mobile social networks. IEEE Trans. Emerg. Top. Comput. Intell. **4**(3), 241–252 (2020)

88. X. Sang, Q. Li, Mimic defense techniques of edge-computing terminal, in *2019 IEEE Fifth International Conference on Big Data Computing Service and Applications (BigDataService)* (2019), pp. 247–251

89. Y. Niu, J. Zhang, A. Wang, C. Chen, An efficient collision power attack on aes encryption in edge computing. IEEE Access **7**, 18734–18748 (2019)

90. Y. Mao, C. You, J. Zhang, K. Huang, K.B. Letaief, A survey on mobile edge computing: the communication perspective. IEEE Commun. Surv. Tutor. **19**(4), 2322–2358 (2017)

91. B. Li, T. Chen, G.B. Giannakis, Secure mobile edge computing in IoT via collaborative online learning. IEEE Trans. Signal Process. **67**(23), 5922–5935 (2019)

92. A. Zimba, C. Hongsong, W. Zhaoshun, Edge aggregation based bayesian modeling of cyber attacks in hypervisor-enabled IAAS cloud networks, in *2017 IEEE 17th International Conference on Communication Technology (ICCT)* (2017), pp. 1312–1317

93. W. Tong, B. Jiang, F. Xu, Q. Li, S. Zhong, Privacy-preserving data integrity verification in mobile edge computing, in *2019 IEEE 39th International Conference on Distributed Computing Systems (ICDCS)* (2019), pp. 1007–1018

94. Deepali, K. Bhushan, DDoS attack defense framework for cloud using fog computing, in *2017 2nd IEEE International Conference on Recent Trends in Electronics, Information Communication Technology (RTEICT)* (2017), pp. 534–538

95. M. Al-Zinati, T. Almasri, M. Alsmirat, Y. Jararweh, A mobile-edge computing bio-surveillance framework for multiple biological attacks detection, in *2019 Sixth International Conference on Internet of Things: Systems, Management and Security (IOTSMS)* (2019), pp. 104–109

96. H. Xu, S. Hao, A. Sari, H. Wang, Privacy risk assessment on email tracking, in *IEEE INFOCOM 2018 - IEEE Conference on Computer Communications 2018*, pp. 2519–2527

97. M. Nasr, R. Shokri, A. Houmansadr, Comprehensive privacy analysis of deep learning: passive and active White-Box inference attacks against centralized and federated learning, in *2019 IEEE Symposium on Security and Privacy (SP)* (IEEE, New York, 2019), pp. 739–753

98. B. Mei, Y. Xiao, R. Li, H. Li, X. Cheng, Y. Sun, Image and attribute based convolutional neural network inference attacks in social networks. IEEE Trans. Netw. Sci. Eng. **7**(2), 869–879 (2018)

99. Daniele Riboni, Linda Pareschi, and Claudio Bettini. JS-reduce: defending your data from sequential background knowledge attacks. IEEE Trans. Depend. Secure Comput. **9**(3), 387–400 (2012)

100. M. Rezvani, A. Ignjatovic, E. Bertino, S. Jha, Secure data aggregation technique for wireless sensor networks in the presence of collusion attacks. IEEE Trans. Depend. Secure Comput. **12**(1), 98–110 (2015)

101. R. Yu, J. Kang, X. Huang, S. Xie, Y. Zhang, S. Gjessing, Mixgroup: accumulative pseudonym exchanging for location privacy enhancement in vehicular social networks. IEEE Trans. Depend. Secure Comput. **13**(1), 93–105 (2016)

102. J. Song, S. Lee, J. Kim, Inference attack on browsing history of twitter users using public click analytics and twitter metadata. IEEE Trans. Depend. Secure Comput. **13**(3), 340–354 (2016)
103. Y. Chen, Y. Nadji, A. Kountouras, F. Monrose, R. Perdisci, M. Antonakakis, N. Vasiloglou, Practical attacks against graph-based clustering, in *Proceedings of the 2017 ACM SIGSAC Conference on Computer and Communications Security, CCS 2017*, Dallas, TX, October 30–November 03, 2017, pp. 1125–1142
104. J. Wang, C. Jiang, L. Gao, S. Yu, Z. Han, Y. Ren, Complex network theoretical analysis on information dissemination over vehicular networks, in *2016 IEEE International Conference on Communications (ICC)* (2016), pp. 1–6
105. M.A. Ferrag, L.A. Maglaras, A. Ahmim, Privacy-preserving schemes for ad hoc social networks: a survey. IEEE Commun. Surv. Tutor. **19**(4), 3015–3045 (2017)
106. B. Ying, D. Makrakis, H.T. Mouftah, Privacy preserving broadcast message authentication protocol for VANETs. J. Netw. Comput. Appl. **36**(5), 1352–1364 (2013)
107. D. Quercia, S. Hailes, Sybil attacks against mobile users: friends and foes to the rescue, in *Proceedings of INFOCOM 2010. 29th IEEE International Conference on Computer Communications, Joint Conference of the IEEE Computer and Communications Societies*, 15–19 March 2010, San Diego, CA (2010), pp. 336–340
108. C. Liu, P. Gao, M.K. Wright, P. Mittal, Exploiting temporal dynamics in sybil defenses, in *Proceedings of the 22nd ACM SIGSAC Conference on Computer and Communications Security*, Denver, CO, October 12–16 (2015), pp. 805–816

Chapter 3
Context-Aware Privacy Preserving in Edge Computing

In edge computing, edge nodes are hierarchically arranged, while data transmission is allowed among edge nodes [1]. Because end devices are the closest to raw data sources, they usually submit requests with sensitive information to the edge nodes. Privacy issues occur during the transmission process. In addition, when an end user sends a request to edge nodes, the end user connects to the closest edge node initially, and the request is passed to the upper-layer edge nodes for further processing when the resources of the initial nodes are exhausted. The resource limitation includes computation, storage capabilities, and the number of users [2]. For example, if a user generates one request to the connected edge node exceeding its computation power, the upper-layer edge node will be involved in the operation. Additionally, the information will be transmitted to the other edge nodes, which might be malicious. Thus, privacy preservation is necessary to prevent privacy leakage from data transition among multiple edge nodes in hierarchical structures [3].

To address the uncovered issues indicated in Chap. 2, we propose a model that focuses on the optimal tradeoff between data utility and customizable privacy protection. We devise a novel Markov decision process (MDP) [4]-based privacy-preserving method (MDP-PPFC) to balance the tradeoff during data communication, particularly for content-aware applications and requests in hierarchical edge-driven structures. In MDP-PPFC, the MDP-based algorithm will provide multistage protection in which the strategy is updated in every time slot. In other words, the multistage selection continues adjusting the strategies until it identifies the best strategies for the initial user requested in finite time slots. We derive the Nash equilibrium (NE) [5] of MDP as the optimal tradeoff. For the purpose of fast convergence, we improve the efficiency of the state-action-reward-state-action (SARSA) reinforcement learning algorithm by cardinality reduction. In this method, cardinality is reduced from n to 2 so that the computational complexity decreases exponentially. Our extensive experiments indicate the performance superiority in terms of efficiency and accuracy.

Our main novelty in this chapter is summarized as follows:

- Devising a dynamic privacy-preserving scheme named MDP-PPFC to provide privacy protection to both content and location. We consider a dynamic hierarchical connection with adaptable adversaries. Moreover, this is an early work to provide long-term privacy protection to both privacy issues in hierarchical edge computing.
- Addressing the identified issues using a reinnovated MDP formulation to establish a multistage game model. The model dynamically approximates the best strategy of the user by the derivation of an exclusive Nash equilibrium (NE). In particular, we obtain the optimal tradeoff by considering the least privacy loss statics and the QoS-based payoff function.
- Using a modified SARSA reinforcement learning algorithm for the purpose of rapid convergence to NE. In addition, the modified SARSA algorithm captures the features in the proposed MDP-PPFC model. Fast convergence can be achieved because of the reduction in cardinality due to n to 2.
- Extensive evaluations are implemented on real-world datasets to demonstrate the superior performance of the proposed algorithms. The evaluation results show significant performance in terms of privacy protection, data utility, and efficiency regarding both the satisfactory threshold and the percentage of sensitive messages. Promisingly, the results provide potential guidance for the design of context-aware application privacy preservation in edge computing.

3.1 System Modeling

In this section, we present our dynamic MDP-based privacy-preserving model in edge computing (MDP-PPFC) environments. The efficiency of privacy preservation in our hybrid model focuses on protecting both location and content from the user end. First, we introduce the model based on MDP, including the system states and state transitions. In addition, we introduce the functionality of the Nash equilibrium in our system to analyze the payoff function in the model. Finally, the problem is formulated into our hybrid model, in which the user and system can maximize the accurate results by finding the tradeoff to protect both privacy issues in a hierarchical edge computing structure. We consider comprehensive modeling to provide high-level privacy for edge computing (Fig. 3.1).

3.1.1 Actions of Adversary

By determining the actions of adversaries, we examine a dynamic adversary model that has limited computing capacity and cannot monitor or investigate user messages. However, unlike the popular adversary model, the proposed model is

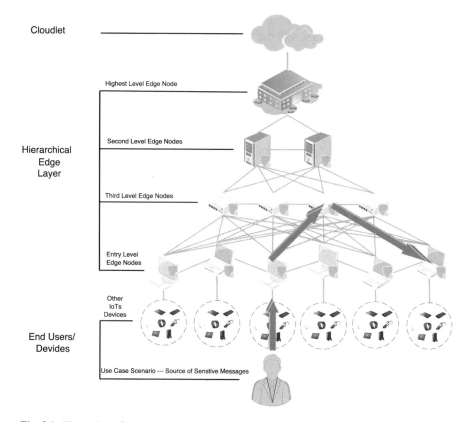

Cloudlet

Hierarchical Edge Layer

Highest Level Edge Node

Second Level Edge Nodes

Third Level Edge Nodes

Entry Level Edge Nodes

Other IoTs Devices

End Users/ Devides

Use Case Scenario --- Source of Senstive Messages

Fig. 3.1 Illustration of content privacy with the MDP-PPFC-based model

designated as a dynamic adversary traversal system with unlimited computing capacity. This dynamic adversary model is not feasible due to limited computing resources. Thus, this intelligent attacker cannot modify or inject any messages. The adversary actively collects information published by users, trying to breach the privacy of location and identity while users defend the adversaries by changing strategies in finite stages.

The enemy's sequence of actions is considered to be the probability of successful eavesdropping. Adversaries not only have limited computing resources to observe user-published messages but are also interested in influencing the possibility of eavesdropping. In particular, we define the adversary behavior in stage t as A_{adv}^t, which indicates the probability that the adversary launches an attack. Therefore, the computational constraints of adversaries are expressed as follows:

$$\sum_t A_{adv}^t \le \Xi, 0 \le A_{adv}^t \le 1 \tag{3.1}$$

where Ξ determines the unlimited computing capacities of the adversary at attacking stage t. When $\Xi \leq t$, we assume the adversary has the capability to eavesdrop all messages in every stage (Table 3.1).

Table 3.1 Table of notations

Notation	Description
A_k	Action space of the player
$\upsilon^{adv} : S_{adv} \mapsto \Delta(A_{adv})$	Adversary policy
$\eta_q \in [0, 1]$	Reinforcement learning algorithm learning rate
Ar^t	Attack result in the last time slot
$\{\upsilon^*_{user}, \upsilon^*_{adv}\}$	Best approach policy
$C(|A|^3|S|^3)$	Computational complexity
U_{ut}	Data utilities
$\eta_q = 1/t$	Decrease the convergence time in the best strategy level
$R(r)$	Function of the message r
$C = \{c^1, c^2, c^3, \dots, c^n\}$	Individual regional nodes
$QoS(A^t_{user})$	Measurement of the overall data utility
$P_{loss}((S^t_{user}, , S^t_{adv}))$	Privacy loss at R_t and ω
$[\Delta(A_{user}), \Delta(A_{adv})]$	Probability as the action spaces of the user and adversary
$\rho(S)$	Set of probability distributions over state
R_k	Stage payoff function of the player
S^t_{adv}	State of the adversary at time slot t
S^t_{user}	State of user at time slot t
$\{c^j, u^j, m^j, t^j\}$	Action
S^t_{user}	State of user at time slot t
$\{c^j, u^j, m^j, t^j\}$	State of user-published messages
(S_{user}, S_{adv})	State spaces
ς'	Subnet of ς that consists of σ messages
$T = \{t^1, t^2, t^3, \dots, t^n\}$	Time slot of communication
$\upsilon^{user} : S_{user} \mapsto \Delta(A_{user})$	User policy
$M = \{m^1, m^2, m^3, \dots, m^n\}$	User-published messages
$U = \{u^1, u^2, u^3, \dots, u^n\}$	Users
$\widehat{G}^{\upsilon^*}(A_r)$	Value of expectation

3.1.2 Problem Formulation

Edge nodes provide all kinds of services within the limitations of their capabilities. For example, a user sends a request to the current linked edge server, such as downloading an American action movie. First, we initially split all edge nodes into individual regional nodes $C = \{c^1, c^2, c^3, \ldots, c^n\}$. Each node corresponds to the area closest to the users, and only one service is available in each region. We use $M = \{m^1, m^2, m^3, \ldots, m^n\}$ to describe the message that the user has published and $U = \{u^1, u^2, u^3, \ldots, u^n\}$ to define the users. To be more accurate, we also divide the time during the communication into time slots as $T = \{t^1, t^2, t^3, \ldots, t^n\}$. Overall, the state when the user publishes messages is described as $\{c^j, u^j, m^j, t^j\}$.

In the game formulation, the message published by the user is an American action movie. Meanwhile, the message received by the new edge node is only a movie request. The game begins during the process as the new node only returns a certain amount of the movie back to the user, and the user returns the message until they find a satisfactory tradeoff. In the MDP description, when the user takes a step (action a) in a situation (state s), the choice of the opponent node (which leads to the next state s') is uncertain. However, the choice is only related to s and a without considering the earlier state and action. In other words, s' is randomly generated according to s and a.

3.1.3 Markov Decision Process (MDP)

The MDP considers the action, and the next state of the system is related to both the current state and current action. A zero-sum game with probabilistic trading and multiple finite stages is the key component of the MDP. For a three-player competitive MDP, we promote the eight-tuple $\{S, A_1, A_2, A_3, R_1, R_2, R_3, \text{Pr}\}$ to define MDP-PPFC, where S is the discrete space, and A_k denotes the action space of player k, where $k = 1, 2, 3$. $R_k \colon S \times A_1 \times A_2 \times A_3 \mapsto R$ is the stage payoff function of player k, where $\mapsto$ denotes the input and output mapping function. $\text{Pr} : S \times A_1 \times A_2 \times A_3 \mapsto \rho$ denotes the probability of the transition map, where $\rho(S)$ is the set of probability distributions over state S. It is important to note that the stage payoff and transition rely on the state of the system and the actions of the players in our model.

3.1.4 System State

For the adversary attack without our model, the adversary collects an instant message that refers to the location or context. In contrast, when the modeled system is active, the end devices and users are a certain departure point, the message request is forwarded to the edge layer, and the end user connects with the initial edge node based on the distance and signal strength. The message request contains the context-aware application or information that the user would like to protect. In this scenario, the system states include the user context, and the adversary can only detect the context-based information with the modification and Markov model from the user end.

In addition, we consider both requests and actions from the adversary because the initial edge node will not be notified of the action and strategy of the adversary. If the initial edge node receives the notification that is returned by the new edge nodes, this implies that the adversary has breached the privacy protection and identified the location of the initial node. To protect location privacy, the initial edge node saves the previous location record that the adversary has targeted or breached. In this case, the notification returned by the new node will be invalid. We denote Ar^t as the attack result in the last time slot t. $Ar^t = 1$ indicates a successful attack by the adversary, and $Ar^t = 0$ indicates an attack failure. Thus, the system states at time t are defined as follows.

$$S^t = \left\{ R_t, Ar^t \right\} \tag{3.2}$$

3.1.5 State Transition

Because of the uncertainty of R_t, the state $(S_1^t, S_2^t, S_3^t, \ldots, S_m^t)$ remains uncertain, but the state is defined by both actions from the users and adversary. Meanwhile, Ar^t is also determined by an independent action defined by the user's behavior. Therefore, we define the state transition as

$$\Pr \left[(S_{user}^t, , S_{adv}^t) \mid (S_m^{t+1}, , S_m^{t+1}), , A_{user}^{t+1}, , A_{adv}^{t+1} \right]$$
$$= \Pr [R_t \mid R_{t+1}] \Pr \left[Ar^t \mid Ar^{t+1}, A_{user}^{t+1}, A_{adv}^{t+1} \right] \tag{3.3}$$
$$= \Pr [R_t \mid R_{t+1}] \Pr \left[Ar^t \mid A_{user}^{t+1}, A_{adv}^{t+1} \right]$$

The second equality is generated because of the attack result AR^t observed at time $t + 1$, which only depends on the actions of the user and adversary in the last stage $t + 1$.

3.1.6 MDP-Based Nash Equilibrium

The Nash equilibrium is one of the most important strategy combinations in game theory. It refers to a strategy combination of edge nodes in which neither edge nodes nor users can benefit from changing the strategy alone, i.e., if no one changes the strategy in combination with another.

The payoff function and transition map are considered based on the states and actions of all players. It also defines the quality of the resulting service between edge nodes and users. The payoff function can be described as

$$
\begin{aligned}
R_{user}&((S_{user}^t,, S_{adv}^t), A_{user}^t,, A_{adv}^t) \\
&= \mathrm{QoS}(A_{user}^t) - \omega \cdot P_{loss}((S_{user}^t,, S_{adv}^t))
\end{aligned}
\tag{3.4}
$$

where $\mathrm{QoS}(A_{user}^t)$ is the measurement of overall data utility with the user content-based service. $P_{loss}((S_{user}^t,, S_{adv}^t))$ is the privacy loss at R_t and ω, which is equivalent to the improvement of the service quality in terms of privacy loss.

In a dynamic game process, we define a strategy as the probability transitions over the action set for any state. In addition, we define a stationary strategy as υ, where $(\upsilon_t = \upsilon)$, i.e., the policy is fixed at time t. In our edge-node-aware context-sensitive game model, we denote the user policy as $\upsilon^{user} : S_{user} \mapsto \Delta(A_{user})$, and the adversary policy can be denoted as $\upsilon^{adv} : S_{adv} \mapsto \Delta(A_{adv})$, where (S_{user}, S_{adv}) defines the state spaces, and $[\Delta(A_{user}), \Delta(A_{adv})]$ is the probability and is defined as the action spaces of the user and adversary.

In this case, we provide a specific state $s \in S$ as the strategy of the users and adversary given the utility of the users. While we focus on a stable strategy, A_{user}^t and A_{adv}^t are determined by policies υ^{user} and υ^{adv}, respectively. Therefore, the utilities can be written as

$$
\mathrm{G}^{\upsilon}(s) = \sum_{t=0} \mathrm{E}[R_{user}((S_{user}^t,, S_{adv}^t), A_{user}^t,, A_{adv}^t) \mid \upsilon^{user}, \upsilon^{adv}, S^0 = s]
\tag{3.5}
$$

$$
\mathrm{G}^{\upsilon}(s) = R_{user}(s, A_{user}^t,, A_{adv}^t) + \sum_{s'} \Pr[s' \mid s, A_{user}^t,, A_{adv}^t] \mathrm{G}^{\upsilon}(s')
\tag{3.6}
$$

Since both the user and adversary follow their best approach policies $\{\upsilon_{user}^*, \upsilon_{adv}^*\}$ to maximize the individual utilities, in this stage, we use the best strategy pair, which is $\upsilon* = \{\upsilon_{user}^* + \upsilon_{adv}^*\}$, and all states $s \in S$.

According to game theory and the NE formulation, given a dynamic zero-sum stochastic game, we define state $s \in S$. The best strategy for pair $\upsilon* = \{\upsilon_{user}^* + \upsilon_{adv}^*\}$ is described as

$$
\begin{cases}
G^{\upsilon^*}(s) \geq G^{\upsilon_{adv}}(s) \\
G^{\upsilon^*}(s) \leq G^{\upsilon_{adv}}(s)
\end{cases}
\tag{3.7}
$$

where $\upsilon_{adv} = \{\upsilon_{user}, , \upsilon_{adv}^*\}$, and $\upsilon_{user} = \{\upsilon_{user}^*, , \upsilon_{adv}\}$, for all υ_{adv} and υ_{user}.

In the context privacy game, the user attempts to protect υ^{user^*} to protect their utilities. Meanwhile, the adversary attempts to minimize their $G^{\upsilon}(s)$ by using υ^{adv^*}. According to Eq. 3.5, we have

$$
G^{\upsilon^*}(s) = \max_{\upsilon_{user}} \min_{\upsilon_{adv}} \left\{ R(s, A_{user}^t, , A_{adv}^t) \right.
$$

$$
\left. + \sum_{s'} \Pr[s' \mid s, A_{user}^t, , A_{adv}^t] G^{\upsilon}(s') \right\}
\tag{3.8}
$$

An exclusive NE is by default in our MDP-PPFC model because [6] has proven that the equilibrium in the dynamic zero-sum game is exclusive.

3.2 System Analysis

3.2.1 QoS Data Utility Measurement

In the MDP-PPFC model, when the users publish messages, we denote $QoS(A_{user}^t)$ as their satisfaction rate. To define the QoS, we use the softmax function to model it. The softmax function assigns decimal probabilities to each class in a multiclass problem. It is also widely used to measure user satisfaction according to the QoS. The softmax function incorporates a power function to add a value of e to polarize both ends. The results of the positive and negative samples will approach 1 and 0, respectively, which provide convenience for the multiclassification, where QoS (A_{user}^t) can be considered the probability of the user satisfaction of class A_{user}^t. Thus, we formulate the QoS function as

$$
QoS(A_{user}^t) = \frac{\exp(\theta_i^t x)}{\sum_{k=1}^{K} \exp(\theta_k^t x)}
\tag{3.9}
$$

where $k \in K$, θ_i and x represent the column vector. The softmax function can make the range of QoS (A_{user}^t) be [0, 1]. To classify the user satisfaction QoS, θ is determined as an unknown parameter, and the optimal parameter is θ_i, which maximizes QoS (A_{user}^t).

3.2.2 Privacy Loss Analysis

In privacy loss measurements, we initially define S as the user message space, where $s_i \in S$ is a series of messages with the location and identity information. When the adversary knows limited information about the private state of the user from the implemented data, the published data will remain private, meaning that all sensitive contexts and the differences between the posterior and prior beliefs about the user in the sensitive context are limited at the current time. In fact, we realize that the adversaries are more concerned with the latest messages updated from the user than the future context. According to the above description, we measure the privacy loss using the context sensitivity and entropy of the information. The sensitivity of context $s_t \in S$ is defined as the sum of the discounted difference between the posterior and prior beliefs of the adversary pilfering the current stage of the sensitive messages. Therefore,

$$\text{Cont}(s) = \sum_{t=0}^{} \sum_{s_i \in S_i} | \Pr[s_t = s_i \mid s_0 = s] - \Pr[s_t = s_i] | \qquad (3.10)$$

where message s_t is defined as the message sensitivity for the quantity of information that the adversary can obtain in current stage s_t.

In addition, we model the privacy loss of the users based on the context sensitivity. When the attacks are initiated and the adversary successfully attacks users' current context, the privacy loss of the current stage is the sensitivity of the current context. Conversely, the privacy loss is null when the users' real content remains as an unknown context for the adversary. Thus, we have the following formulation to isolate the attack:

$$P_{loss}((S_{user}^t, , S_{adv}^t), A_{user}^t, , A_{adv}^t) = \text{Cont}(s_t) A R^{t+1} \qquad (3.11)$$

After we have defined the privacy loss, we mention ω in Eq. 3.3, which denotes the service quality improvement for each unit of the privacy loss. Two situations are compared: the adversary can access all raw user sensing data, and the adversary knows nothing. In our MDP-PPFC model, we assume the common case that the adversary has background knowledge regardless of the prior belief of the user context. For example, the adversary can study or approximate the user behavior pattern based on a previous MDP transition. We can obtain that the stage payoff for the adversary is the negative of Eq. 3.3 after substituting Eqs. 3.8, 3.9, and 3.10 back into Eq. 3.3.

In general, the user regularly updates their message during the lifecycle of the service, such as running applications and continuing mutualization with edge nodes. Therefore, it is an infinite stage in which the MDP-PPFC plays a role in the entire edge computing structure. In edge computing, this causes immediate damage to the user, especially when one processes large amounts of private messages. Thus, we formulate the user utility as the expected sum of payoffs in every stage.

$$U_{ut} = E\left[\sum_{t=0} R(Ar((S_{user}^t,, S_{adv}^t), A_{user}^t,, A_{adv}^t))\right] \qquad (3.12)$$

In MDP-PPFC, we aim to find the best defense strategy against attacks from the adversary, which corresponds to finding the maximum U_{ut} while the adversary is aimed at the opposite strategy.

3.3 Reinforcement Learning in Optimal Defense Strategy

Reinforcement learning adopts the method of learning while obtaining samples. It not only updates its model after obtaining samples by using the current model to guide the next action but also updates the model after the next action is rewarded. The process iterates and repeats until the model converges. During the process of reinforcement learning, in the existing model, whether the selection of the next step is the best for the model is determined. SARSA is one of the on-policy reinforcement learning algorithms to obtain decision-making during the MDP.

Based on the problem statement in Sect. 3.1, we modify the SARSA reinforcement learning algorithm to obtain the exclusive NE result of a zero-sum multistage game in our proposed MDP-PPFC model. In this section, we first introduce a fast convergence reinforcement learning algorithm to monitor computational complexity by reducing cardinality from n to 2. In addition, we analyze the best strategy generations with both limited and unlimited computing capabilities by using the exclusive NE point.

3.3.1 Fast Convergence Reinforcement Learning

To achieve better and more accurate NE point results in our dynamic multistage zero-sum MDP, we apply reinforcement learning algorithms to our model. However, we need to modify the existing learning algorithms because they are not perfectly suited in our scenario. Moreover, we focus on using this modified SARSA algorithm to determine the NE point by solving an equivalent problem.

First, we define $\widehat{G}^{v^*}(A_r)$ as the value of expectation from $G_{user}^{v^*}(s)$, where $s = \{Ar, R\}$. After this definition, we can clear M. Therefore, we express $\widehat{G}^{v^*}(A_r)$ as

$$\widehat{G_{user}}^{v^*}(A_r) = E\left[R_{user}(s, A^{v^*}) + \sum_{A_r'}(Pr[Ar' \mid A^{v^*}]\widehat{G}^{v^*}(Ar'))\right] \qquad (3.13)$$

where $A^{v^*} = \left\{A_{user}^{v^*}, A_{adv}^{v^*}\right\}$ denotes the best action after the v^* strategy.

As the value of Ar only has three values, we now reduce the cardinality from our scenario of $|\ s\ |$ to 3. Therefore, we obtain the best strategy pair υ^* to address the equivalent problem.

$$\upsilon^* = \max_{\upsilon_{user}} \min_{\upsilon_{adv}} \mathrm{E}\left[R_{user}(s, A^{\upsilon^*}) + \sum_{A'_r}(\Pr[\mathrm{Ar}' \mid A^{\upsilon^*}]\widehat{G}^{\upsilon^*}(\mathrm{Ar}')) \right] \qquad (3.14)$$

Following Eqs. 3.12 and 3.13, $\widehat{G_{user}}^{\upsilon^*}(\mathrm{A_r})$ can determine the best strategy of υ^*. We then modified the updating rule from the class SARSA algorithm to define our $\widehat{G_{user}}^{\upsilon^*}(\mathrm{A_r})$.

$$\widehat{G}^{q+1}(\mathrm{Ar}) = (1 - \eta_{q+1})\widehat{G}^q(\mathrm{Ar})$$
$$+ \eta_{q+1}\mathrm{E}\left[R(s, A^t_{user},, A^t_{adv}) + \widehat{G}^q(\mathrm{Ar}')\right] \qquad (3.15)$$

where $\eta_q \in [0, 1]$ denotes the algorithm learning rate. We also denote $\eta_q = 1/t$ to decrease the convergence time at the best strategy level. During the update process, $\widehat{G}^{q+1}(\mathrm{Ar})$ is designated as the approximate value of $\widehat{G}^{\upsilon^*}(\mathrm{A_r})$ after certain rounds of updates.

The computational complexity is set as $C(|A|^3|S|^3)$ in the traditional SARSA learning algorithm. However, in our MDP-PPFC model, we proved that the action of cardinality was reduced from n to 2. Hence, the computational complexity is correspondingly reduced to $C(2^3|S|^3)$. Because the cardinality of action A in MDP is generally heavy, our reduction in the cardinality is significant in boosting the performance.

Algorithm 1 Fast convergence reinforcement learning algorithm

---

Require:
    The edge dynamic multistage zero-sum game
Ensure:
    The best game strategy α^*;
1: $t = 0, Ar = 0$;
2: $\widehat{G}^q(\mathrm{Ar}) = 1, Ar = 0$;
3: $\widehat{G}^q(\mathrm{Ar}) = 1, Ar = 0.5$;
4: $\widehat{G}^q(\mathrm{Ar}) = 1, Ar = 1$;
5: Initialization of the strategy pair $\{\alpha_{user}, \alpha_{adv}\}$;
6: **repeat**;
7: Selection of current action pair $\{\alpha_{user}, \alpha_{adv}\}$;
8: Action start;
9: Update value of Ar^{q+1};
10: Update State vale of $\widehat{G}^q(\mathrm{Ar})$;
11: Update α_{q+1} as best strategy in $\widehat{G}^q(\mathrm{Ar})$;
12: Next stage with $q \leftarrow q + 1$;
13: **until** Converge;

3.3.2 The Best Strategy with Unlimited Computing Capabilities

In our MDP-FFPC model, to obtain the state value of $\widehat{G}^q(\mathrm{Ar})$ at stage q, we need to solve the NE in the multistage game. After submitting Eqs. 3.2, 3.3, 3.8, 3.9, and 3.10 into Eq. 3.13, we gather the NE minimax problem as follows:

$$\max_{\upsilon_{user}} \min_{\upsilon_{adv}} \left\{ \frac{2e^{(-\gamma(A^P_{user}-\delta))}}{1+e^{(-\gamma(A^P_{user}-\delta))}} - R(r)A^t_{adv}A^t_{user} - 1 \right\}$$

s.t.

$$\sum_t A^t_{adv} \leq \kappa \qquad\qquad (3.16)$$

$$0 \leq A^t_{adv} \leq 1,, \forall_t$$

$$0 \leq A^t_{user} \leq 1,, \forall_t$$

where $R(r)$ denotes the function of the message r in $R(r) = \omega RSen(r) + (\widehat{G}^{\upsilon^*}(\mathrm{A_r}' = 0) - \widehat{G}^{\upsilon^*}(\mathrm{A_r}' = 1))$. The values of $\upsilon^*(Ar' = 0)$ and $\widehat{G}^{\upsilon^*}(\mathrm{A_r}' = 1)$ remain the same, which $R(r)$ relies on message r. Based on these analyses, we can observe that $\widehat{G}^{\upsilon^*}(\mathrm{A_r}' = 0) > \widehat{G}^{\upsilon^*}(\mathrm{A_r}' = 1)$. Thus, we conclude the function of the message $R(r) > 0$ as $RSen(r) \geq 0$.

To solve problem in Eq. 3.15, considering our scenario in this chapter, we assume υ_{user} is fixed for a constant value. In a previous study, we proved $R(r) > 0$, the adversary to filch message κ to attach a minimum value; thus, the problem becomes

$$\max_{\upsilon_{user},\sigma,\varsigma'} \left\{ \frac{2e^{(-\gamma(A^P_{user}-\delta))}}{1+e^{(-\gamma(A^P_{user}-\delta))}} - R(r)A^t_{user} - 1 \right\}$$

s.t.

$$0 \leq A^t_{user} \leq 1,, \forall_t \qquad\qquad (3.17)$$

$$A^t_{adv} \leq \sigma, \forall_t \in \varsigma'$$

$$A^t_{user} \geq \sigma, \forall_t \in \{\varsigma \mid \varsigma'\}$$

where ς' is a subnet of ς that consists of σ messages. We can derive the closed form for the best strategy υ_{user} by that given ς'.

3.3.3 The Best Strategy with Limited Computing Capabilities

In the previous analysis, we assume the adversary has limited computing capabilities and limited bandwidth, and the adversary can only filch the message on their best strategy. In this subsection, we analyze the situation with the adversary come with unlimited computing capabilities and unlimited access for edge node messages during the attack. At this point, the scenario has changed. However, our modified SARSA Algorithm 1 can still be applied and reformulated to

$$\max_{\upsilon_{user}} \left\{ \frac{2e^{(-\gamma(A_{user}^{p}-\delta))}}{1+e^{(}-\gamma(A_{user}^{p}-\delta))} - R(r)\max_{\upsilon^{*}} A_{adv}^{t}A_{user}^{t} - 1 \right\}$$

s.t. $\qquad\qquad\qquad\qquad\qquad\qquad\qquad\qquad\qquad$ (3.18)

$$0 \leq A_{adv}^{t} \leq 1, , \forall_{t}$$

$$0 \leq A_{user}^{t} \leq 1, , \forall_{t}$$

where constraint κ for A_{adv}^{t} has been removed from the equation. In addition, we can observe that $\max_{\upsilon^{*}} A_{adv}^{t}A_{user}^{t} = A_{user}^{t}$. Hence, the formation changes to

$$\max_{\upsilon_{user}} \left\{ \frac{2e^{(-\gamma(A_{user}^{p}-\delta))}}{1+e^{(}-\gamma(A_{user}^{p}-\delta))} - R(r)A_{user}^{t} - 1 \right\}$$

s.t. $\qquad\qquad\qquad\qquad\qquad\qquad\qquad\qquad\qquad$ (3.19)

$$0 \leq A_{adv}^{t} \leq 1, , \forall_{t}$$

$$0 \leq A_{user}^{t} \leq 1, , \forall_{t}$$

where we can obtain the closed form expression for the best strategy υ_{user}.

3.4 Performance Evaluation

In this section, we conduct a series of simulations to test the effectiveness of the proposed MDP-PPFC model from three aspects. For the character of edge nodes, we define the lowest level of edge nodes in the edge hierarchical structure, such as user mobile phones and actuators. First, we evaluate the payoff changes with an increasing satisfaction threshold, followed by the privacy loss changes in terms of the percentage of sensitive messages. Finally, the efficiency of the fast convergence reinforcement learning algorithm is compared with the classic version. To verify these results, we use the latest version of the Yelp dataset [7], which contains approximately 6 million user reviews and more than 188,000 businesses in 10 metropolitan areas worldwide. With such a large amount of information in the dataset, we mainly focus on the information of business, reviews, and users. These elements correspond to location, user action, and identity in MDP-PPFC. We define user actions according to the real-time dataset to simulate and evaluate the performances of our model.

In the first two sets of experiments, we compare MDP-PPFC with two primary algorithms, the static strategy and shortsighted strategy. In the shortsighted strategy, a user only focuses on maximizing the current payoff instead of the future payoff. In the static strategy, we set the same granularity ($\frac{1}{n}$) for all actions. Additionally, to demonstrate the advantage of the modified SARSA algorithm, we compare the convergence speed between the classic SARSA algorithm and the modified SARSA algorithm.

For the parameters, we have the following default parameter settings unless specific statements are given. A satisfactory setting is 8, and we set the identity or location privacy as 5 for the number of messages to re-identify the edge nodes (locations). Initially, we use a random algorithm to select 15,000 records with valid content, including the ID, location, and reviews, from the dataset. We use a trained dataset to compare the privacy protection level and data utilities between our proposed algorithm and the two static algorithms. To provide experimental evaluation, the algorithms are implemented on a Java platform and integrated on macOS High Sierra with an Intel i5 3.1 GHz processor with 8 GB RAM.

3.4.1 Iteration Times Evaluation

We evaluate the number of iterations in both limited and unlimited computing capabilities. Moreover, we also compare the performance when the edge node faces the same situation in dynamic attacks by adversaries. In Figs. 3.2, 3.3, 3.4, 3.5, 3.6, 3.7, we conduct a series of experimental results in three different cities by comparing them with three different algorithms, including the MDP-PPFC model.

In Figs. 3.2, 3.3, and 3.4, the sum of payoff values of the static algorithm is low and stable for all three cities. All the values are under 0.5, which is impractical. For MDP-PPFC and the shortsighted algorithm, the sum of payoff values sharply increases when the number of iterations falls in the interval of [0, 200]. After 200 iterations, they all converge, while MDP-PPFC converges to a higher value in all cases. The values of MDP-PPFC are more than 0.25 higher than those of the shortsighted algorithm. The convergence values of MDP-PPFC are 2.05, 2.23, and 3.48, respectively.

In Figs. 3.5, 3.6, and 3.7, the trend of the curves is similar to the previous trend. The sum of payoff values of the static algorithm is low and stable for all three cities. All the values are no more than 0.02. For both MDP-PPFC and the shortsighted algorithm, the sum of payoff values sharply increases when the number of iterations falls in the interval of [0, 200]. After 200 iterations, they all converge, while MDP-PPFC converges to a higher value in all cases. The values of MDP-PPFC are approximately 0.03 higher than those of the shortsighted algorithm. The convergence values of MDP-PPFC are 0.152, 0.173, and 0.348.

As shown in the figures, the shortsighted algorithm and our proposed MDP-PPFC have much better performance than the static algorithm. The major reason is that shortsighted algorithms do not consider the future payoff but ours does. Moreover,

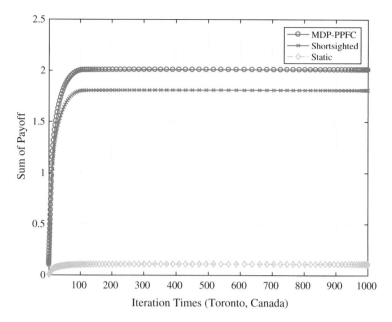

Fig. 3.2 Evaluation of the number of iterations with limited computing capabilities for Toronto, Ontario, Canada

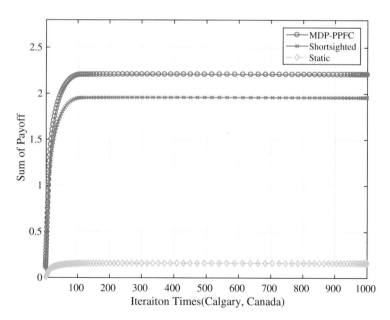

Fig. 3.3 Evaluation of the number of iterations with limited computing capabilities for Calgary, Alberta, Canada

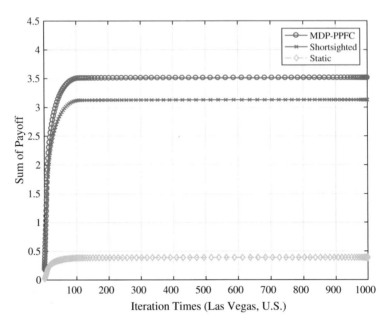

Fig. 3.4 Evaluation of the number of iterations with limited computing capabilities for Las Vegas, Nevada, USA

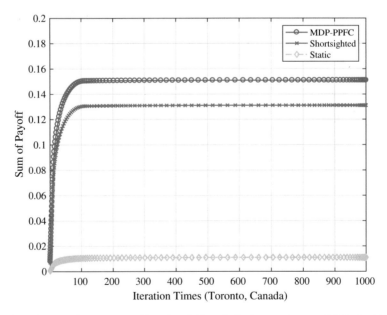

Fig. 3.5 Evaluation of the number of iterations with unlimited computing capabilities for Toronto, Ontario, Canada

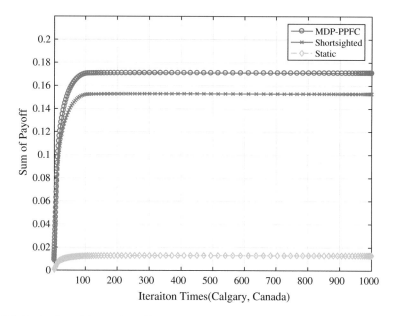

Fig. 3.6 Evaluation of the number of iterations with unlimited computing capabilities for Calgary, Alberta, Canada

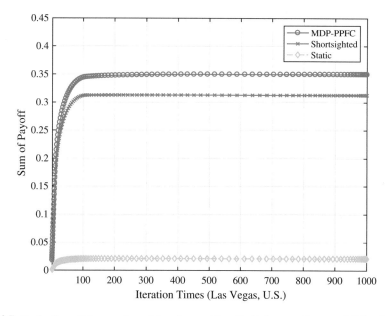

Fig. 3.7 Evaluation of the number of iterations with unlimited computing capabilities for Las Vegas, Nevada, USA

the shortsighted algorithm only focuses on maximizing the current payoff. In addition, we can conclude that with the improvement of the adversary computing capabilities, the edge node payoff will decrease. Moreover, when the adversary reaches the state of unlimited computing capabilities, the edge node revenue will decrease sharply.

3.4.2 Payoff Changes Evaluation

Figures 3.8, 3.9, 3.10, 3.11, 3.12, 3.13 show the sum of payoff changes with increasing satisfactory threshold and sensitive messages for three representative cities from the Yelp dataset: Toronto and Calgary from Canada and Las Vegas from the USA.

In Figs. 3.8, 3.9, and 3.10, we can determine that the payoff with a small satisfactory threshold from the beginning is relatively high and similar for all three algorithms. The values decrease in an exponential manner with an increase in the satisfactory threshold. Let us take Toronto as an example. The payoff values of all three algorithms start from approximately 4.74. The static threshold decreases to nearly 0 when the satisfactory threshold is 10. This problem occurs because the QoS

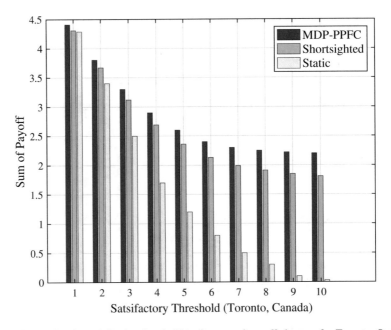

Fig. 3.8 Increasing the satisfaction threshold in the sum of payoff changes for Toronto, Ontario, Canada

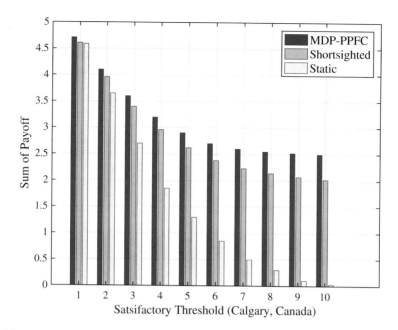

Fig. 3.9 Increasing the satisfaction threshold in the sum of payoff changes for Calgary, Alberta, Canada

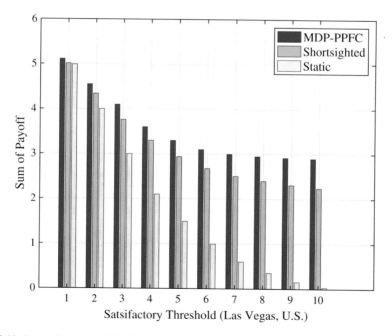

Fig. 3.10 Increasing the satisfaction threshold in the sum of payoff changes for Las Vegas, Nevada, USA

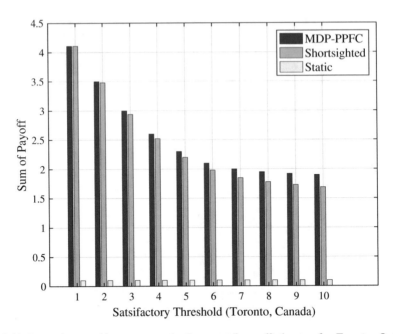

Fig. 3.11 Increasing sensitive messages in the sum of payoff changes for Toronto, Ontario, Canada

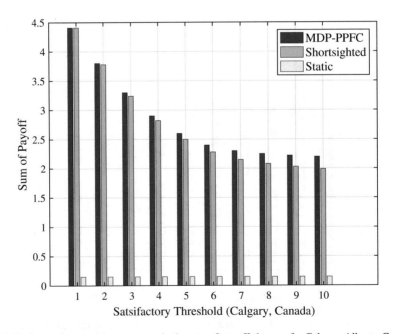

Fig. 3.12 Increasing sensitive messages in the sum of payoff changes for Calgary, Alberta, Canada

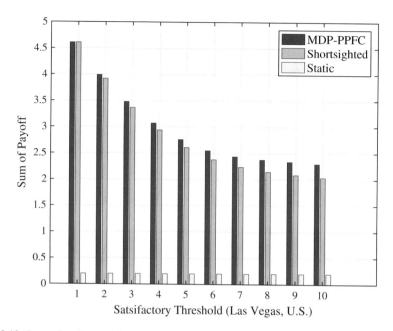

Fig. 3.13 Increasing the sensitive messages in the sum of payoff changes for Las Vegas, Nevada, USA

is large for a small satisfactory threshold. MDP-PPFC converges to 2.61, which has the best performance among all three algorithms.

Figures 3.11, 3.12, and 3.13 illustrate the increase in the sensitive messages when the sum of payoff changes. The payoff of the MDP-PPFC algorithm and shortsighted algorithm decreases with increasing sensitive messages within the entire system. In this case, the payoff value of the static algorithm remains at the low level of approximately 0.17. For the static algorithm, no matter what action the adversary takes, the quality of service remains at the same level, which leads to a fixed payoff, as shown in the figure. In contrast, MDP-PPFC and the shortsighted algorithm have the same greatest payoff value, for instance, 4.43 in Calgary. However, the shortsighted algorithm has a relatively larger decreasing rate, which is why MDP-PPFC is better overall. MDP-PPFC converges to 2.26 after the number of sensitive messages reaches 8. In the other two algorithms, the reason for the decrease in payoff is that when the percentage of sensitive information is high, there will be more privacy loss. In addition, the results also show that when the percentage is small, the difference between the proposed algorithm and the shortsighted algorithm is smaller than that when the percentage is large. Less impact for the user action is conducted when the messages contain less information.

Based on the results, Figs. 3.8, 3.9, 3.10, 3.11, 3.12, 3.13 show that the future payoff impact is negligible if the message contains a small amount of sensitive information for a low satisfaction threshold. However, in real-time edge computing and most real-world network structures, especially in this big data era, an increasing number of sensitive messages are being generated every second. Users are getting used to saving their bank details, personal information, and other personal-related or business-related information in edge nodes or the cloud, which makes our proposed algorithm more practical and realistic. Overall, the MDP-PPFC algorithm has better performances than the other two algorithms.

3.4.3 Privacy Loss Changes

Continuing from the above simulation, in this set of experiments, we obtain satisfactory results in terms of the privacy loss varying with the percentage of sensitive messages and satisfaction. To simulate the results for the privacy loss changes in terms of both sensitive messages and satisfaction thresholds, we analyze and assume the experimental environment in two folds: density of privacy metrics of location and identity privacy. In addition, the edge nodes can choose anonymity, partial release, or full release to publish sensitive information.

We assume the adversary can obtain accurate statistics for the public information and locations, as the adversary can access these information service providers or access sensitive messages through the website. More specifically, we assume adversaries use the necessary information and prepare to launch attacks. Therefore, we define $\mu_m = \frac{n_i^l}{N^l}$ for the location density and identity density as $v_m = \frac{n_i^d}{N^d}$, where n_i^d is the quantity of edge nodes publishing at region μ_i and n_i^l denotes the quantity of location information publishing in region v_i.

In privacy metrics location and identity setting, we assume the adversary filches the data provided by the unit region. We measure the privacy loss of the user with the entropy metric. To generalize the entropy, it is calculated for each service and each edge node. To better measure the location and identity privacy, we define the corresponding entropies as Eqs. 3.20 and 3.21.

$$e_i^l = - \sum_{f_l} \mu_{f_l} \Pr[f = f_l] log_2 \Pr[f = f_l] \tag{3.20}$$

$$e_d^l = - \sum_{f_d} v_{f_d} \Pr[f = f_d] log_2 \Pr[f = f_d] \tag{3.21}$$

where μ_{f_l} and v_{f_d} denote the location and identity privacy to obtain normalized entropy. The possibility that the user publishes a message containing location information of service f_l is $\Pr[f = f_l]$. Both entropy e_i^l and e_d^l describe the uncertainties of the adversary about the user inside a unit region.

In Figs. 3.14, 3.15, 3.16, 3.17, 3.18, 3.19, we evaluate the same three cities to confirm that MDP-PPFC has significantly superior performances compared to the other two algorithms.

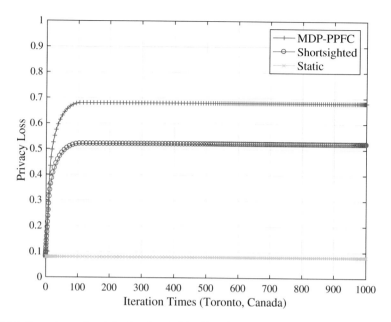

Fig. 3.14 Percentage of satisfaction threshold with privacy loss changes for Toronto, Ontario, Canada

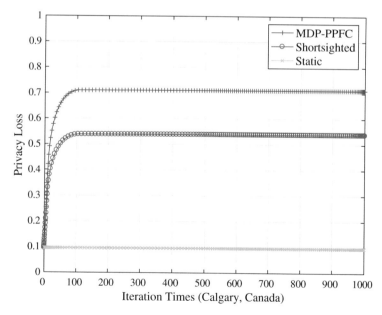

Fig. 3.15 Percentage of satisfaction threshold with privacy loss changes for Calgary, Alberta, Canada

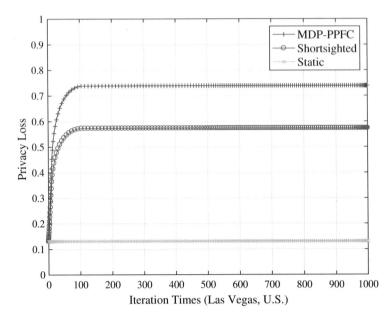

Fig. 3.16 Percentage of satisfaction threshold with privacy loss changes for Las Vegas, Nevada, USA

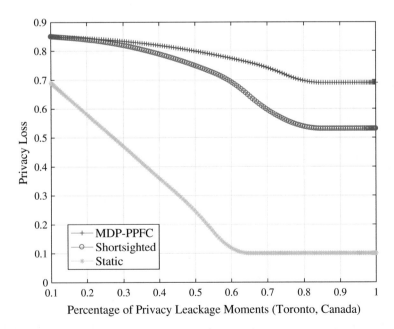

Fig. 3.17 Percentage of sensitive messages with privacy loss changes for Toronto, Ontario, Canada

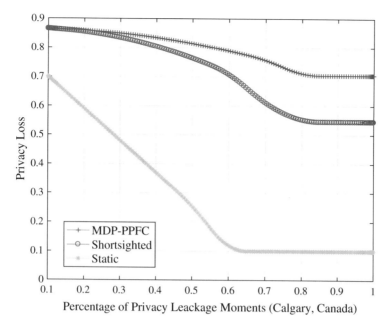

Fig. 3.18 Percentage of sensitive messages with privacy loss changes for Calgary, Alberta, Canada

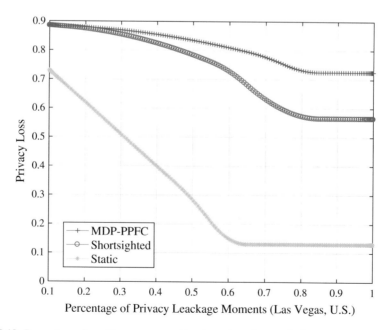

Fig. 3.19 Percentage of sensitive messages with privacy loss changes for Las Vegas, Nevada, USA

When considering privacy preservation, to prevent tracking by the adversaries, the user can select to publish the messages with anonymity, partial release, and full release. We separate all of the edge node zones, and the published messages can only be defined in one of these zones, including both density and privacy metrics of the location and identity.

In Figs. 3.14, 3.15, and 3.16, privacy loss is measured in a reciprocal way so that greater values are less privacy loss. Therefore, it is clear that the privacy loss of MDP-PPFC is the least of the three methods. The evaluation values fall in the range of 0.7 ± 0.02 for different cities, which are approximately 0.18 higher than the values of the shortsighted algorithm. The static algorithm has a constant privacy loss of 0.08, which is in line with reality.

In Figs. 3.17, 3.18, and 3.19, the static algorithm begins relatively low ([0.7, 0.72]) and quickly converges to a lower constant ([0.09, 0.12]). In addition, the static algorithm has a significant decrease in privacy loss with the increase in the percentage of privacy leakage instances. In the case of MDP-PPFC, the decrease in the privacy loss value is at most 0.16, and the values finally approach 0.71 ± 0.01. Although the shortsighted algorithm has the same starting point of 0.86, it decreases at a faster rate and converges in the interval of [0.51, 0.58]. MDP-PPFC considers the long-term future payoff and performs better than the other two algorithms in the dynamic strategy. In fact, smaller message percentages result in less privacy leakage.

3.4.4 Convergence Speed Evaluation

The comparison illustrated in this subsection is between the modified SARSA algorithm and the classic SARSA algorithm. Figures 3.20, 3.21, and 3.22 demonstrate the iteration time of the cumulative distribution function across three different cities and two different countries. We use a semilog coordinate axis, where the x-axis is log-based, to better clarify the comparison. For all three cities, the number of iterations of MDP-PPFC is within $[10^2, 10^3]$, except for Las Vegas, in which there are small overflow values. However, if we use the classic SARSA algorithm, the number of iterations peaks in the range of $[10^5, 10^6]$. As shown in Fig. 3.9, the number of iterations is almost five orders of magnitudes faster for our modified SARSA algorithm and is, therefore, much faster than the classic algorithm. The acceleration is due to the significant cardinality decrease from n to 2.

3.5 Summary

To conclude this chapter, we study the context privacy problem during data communication between the user and multiple edge nodes. The efficiency of edge computing increases the risk of sensitive information leakage and puts both location

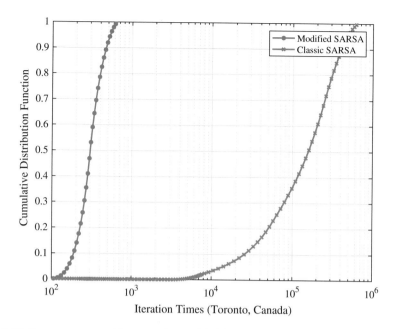

Fig. 3.20 Convergence speed between the modified SARSA and classic SARSA algorithm for Toronto, Ontario, Canada

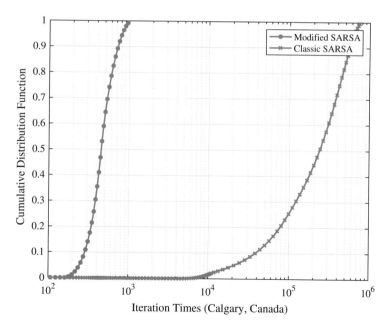

Fig. 3.21 Convergence speed between the modified SARSA and classic SARSA algorithm for Calgary, Alberta, Canada

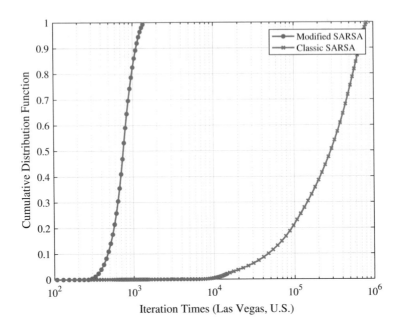

Fig. 3.22 Convergence speed between the modified SARSA and classic SARSA algorithm for Las Vegas, Nevada, USA

and identity privacy under great threats. To solve this issue, we provide a dynamic method to protect user privacy while maintaining data utility at a high-quality standard. We propose a multistage zero-sum game between the users and adversary while formulating the MDP-PPFC model built upon the Markov decision process. We discuss the payoff and privacy loss during the process and thereby obtain the optimal tradeoff. Furthermore, we provide corresponding evaluation results and theoretical analysis of a real-world dataset to test the effectiveness and feasibility of the proposed model.

References

1. F. Bonomi, R. Milito, P. Natarajan, J. Zhu, *Fog Computing: A Platform for Internet of Things and Analytics* (Springer International Publishing, Cham, 2014), pp. 169–186
2. Q. Wang, Y. Zhang, X. Lu, Z. Wang, Z. Qin, K. Ren, Real-time and spatio-temporal crowd-sourced social network data publishing with differential privacy. IEEE Trans. Depend. Secure Comput. **15**(4), 591–606 (2018)
3. Y. Qu, S. Yu, W. Zhou, S. Peng, G. Wang, K. Xiao, Privacy of things: emerging challenges and opportunities in wireless internet of things. IEEE Wirel. Commun. **25**(6), 91–97 (2018)
4. M. Abu Alsheikh, D.T. Hoang, D. Niyato, H. Tan, S. Lin, Markov decision processes with applications in wireless sensor networks: a survey. IEEE Commun. Surv. Tutor. **17**(3), 1239–1267 (thirdquarter 2015)

5. Z. Zhou, M. Dong, K. Ota, R. Shi, Z. Liu, T. Sato, Game-theoretic approach to energy-efficient resource allocation in device-to-device underlay communications. IET Commun. **9**(3), 375–385 (2015)
6. V. Srivastava, J. Neel, A.B. Mackenzie, R. Menon, L.A. Dasilva, J.E. Hicks, J.H. Reed, R.P. Gilles, Using game theory to analyze wireless ad hoc networks. IEEE Commun. Surv. Tutor. **7**(4), 46–56 (fourth 2005)
7. Yelp 12th round dataset. https://www.yelp.com/dataset. Accessed October 2018

Chapter 4
Location-Aware Privacy Preserving in Edge Computing

Edge computing migrates computing to the end user. It directly processes and makes decisions on the data locally [1]. To a certain extent, similar to cloud computing, it avoids the long-distance transmission of data in the network and reduces the risk of privacy leakage. However, due to the users' real-time data obtained by edge nodes, a large number of sensitive privacy data can be obtained by adversaries [2]. The methodologies ensures the usage of the service without disclosing their sensitive location information have proposed higher requirements for privacy protection algorithms in edge computing [3]. Although some data privacy-preserving methods or algorithms are promoted, it is impractical for traditional privacy-preserving techniques to directly address the identified problem in an appropriate manner [4].

Motivated by this, in this chapter, to obtain an optimal tradeoff with high accuracy and efficiency, we propose a dynamic dual-scheme ϵ-customized differential privacy model (DDSDP) based on software-defined edge computing services. Software-defined edge computing flexibly and dynamically provides the network with programmability and privacy protection. In the proposed model, we use dual schemes to obtain tradeoff optimization. First, we start from the edge node clustering approach. This approach brings the user into edge computing services by connecting with a group of edge nodes instead of one stable service provider, while it increases the difficulty when adversaries approach their attacks. We customize ϵ-differential privacy based on the distance between clustered edge nodes. Moreover, we develop a QoS-based mapping function to measure data utilities and privacy protection levels. Our extensive experiments dynamically demonstrate the efficiency and accuracy.

The main novelty of this chapter can be summarized as follows:

- We propose a dual-scheme ϵ-customized differential privacy model to preserve location-aware privacy data for users. We consider a dynamic clustering method to provide first scheme protection for the location-aware data from users to edge nodes. This prevents direct attacks from adaptable adversaries. Moreover, we modify affinity propagation algorithms to improve the efficiency of the clustering approach while providing optimum privacy protection.

- We identify our second scheme with the ϵ-customized protection method with a modified Laplacian mechanism in terms of adding noise into the edge node cluster. We devise a QoS-based function to map the distance of the privacy protection level. DDSDP aims to upgrade data utilities with lower privacy budgets.
- We conduct extensive experiments on a real-world dataset to demonstrate the proposed model. The evaluation results show significant performances in terms of data utilities and privacy protection level.

Furthermore, we analyze two common attacking methods that are widely used by adversaries to attack location-aware data from the edge computing paradigm.

Wormhole Attack

A wormhole attack is a serious attack that can be initiated even if all entities in the communication guarantee authenticity and confidentiality. In this attack, an attacker establishes a private channel between two conspiring malicious nodes that transfers data groupings recorded at a location in the network to another location on the network. To deal with wormhole attacks, methods such as the grid clustering routing algorithm (GCA) have been proposed by J. Zhang et al. [5] and widely deployed in industrial IoT.

DDoS Attack

Another common attacking method in SDN-enabled edge computing is the DDoS attack, which exists in the communication layer. It blocks the transmission of radio signals according to the location service provider [6]. Two types of active interference attacks: continuous interference, i.e., total interference on all transmissions; intermittent interference, in which edge devices periodically send or receive data groupings. The goal of continuous interference is to block all communication transmissions, while the goal of intermittent interference is to reduce the performance of communication [7]. For example, in an edge computing-based smart fire detection system, it would have detected abnormal changes in gas levels in the environment and called the fire brigade in an emergency. An attacker makes the system unreliable by intermittently interfering with the transmission between edge devices and edge devices to base stations. In this case, if the attacker uses continuous interference on location-based edge nodes, the system will stop servicing [8]. Some literature studies [9] have investigated the possibility and effectiveness of DoS attacks against various transport protocols, including Bluetooth. In addition to active interference attacks, an attacker may use malicious edge nodes to initiate a DoS attack and insert an edge device or router that deliberately violates the communication protocol to generate conflicts or interfere with communication.

4.1 System Modeling

In this section, we present our dual-schemeϵ-differential privacy-preserving (DDSDP) scheme in the SDN-enabled edge computing service, as shown in Fig. 4.1. This dual-scheme model focuses on protecting location-aware privacy content between users and edge nodes. We first introduce a modified control layer from SDN infrastructure. This new control layer aims to provide a dynamic clustering solution that relies on real transmission. Each cluster creation is based on the modified affinity propagation (AP) clustering method. In this approach, adversaries cannot determine the source of the initially connected edge node as the clusters are dynamically updated. Therefore, this clustering approach creates privacy protection. Moreover, we present a modified Laplacian mechanism and add Laplacian noise to increase the protection level. We use the QoS mapping method to measure the data utilities and privacy protection level. Thus, the ultimate dual protection of privacy in terms of privacy level and data utility has been created in SDN-enabled edge computing services.

4.1.1 Adversaries Attack Formulation

The efficiency of the adversary attack model of location-aware privacy in the edge computing model is determined by the amount of information that adversaries can obtain from the user's location privacy data after the location information is published. The location data collected by the adversaries can be summarized in a set of spatiotemporal data from user $\{r : r = (p, t)\}$, where r determined one location data collected by an adversary, P defined the location data for the users, and t determined the timing for the data that were collected. Furthermore, sensitive location data that expose users' privacy also form a set as $\{s_1, s_2, \ldots, s_n\}$, where s_i represents the ith position after numbering.

According to the location data collected, adversaries can infer users' privacy information by speculating the probability p that the user is in a sensitive position s_i at time t. To quantify the location data obtained by the adversary to infer the user at a certain sensitive location, we define that the location data published by users at any time t does not disclose the Δ privacy of users in a sensitive location.

Definition 1 (Δ Privacy of Location-Aware Data) □

At any time t', use $P\left\{U_i^{t'}\right\}$ to express the probability rate that the user at position s_i mats the time of t'. In addition, we use L_t to define the location data that the adversary collects at time t. Thus, we have

$$P\left\{U_i^{t'} \mid L_t\right\} - P\left\{U_i^{t'}\right\} \le \Delta \tag{4.1}$$

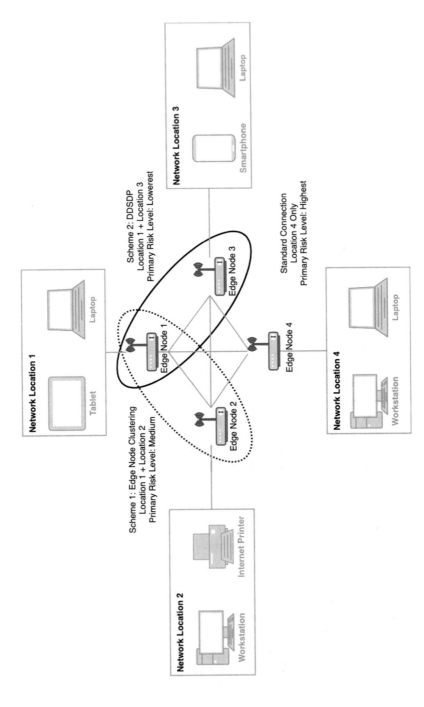

Fig. 4.1 Overview of the DDSDP approach within SDN-enabled edge computing

where Δ is the privacy requirement given by the user, $P\left\{U_i^{t'} \mid L_t\right\}$ defines that the adversary collects the location data before the user's time t and infers the posterior probability of the user's sensitive location s_i at time t', and $P\{U_i\}$ is a prior probability for adversaries to speculate that the user is in a sensitive position s_i. Definition 1 implies that the user location data collected by the adversary are not allowed to exceed more information than Δ for the attacker to infer the user sensitive location. Thus, after obtaining the user's position sequence, the difference between the posterior probability and the prior probability that the user is in a certain sensitive position at a certain time is less than Δ. At any time t', the prior information of the user's location grasped by the adversary is $-\sum_i P\left\{U_i^{t'}\right\} log P\left\{U_i^{t'}\right\}$. Therefore, the quantity of user location privacy data in edge nodes that are exposed to adversaries can be calculated as follows:

$$
\begin{aligned}
Comp(s) = &\sum_i P\left\{U_i^{t'}\right\} log P\left\{U_i^{t'}\right\} \\
&- \sum_i P\left\{U_i^{t'} \mid L_t\right\} log P\left\{U_i^{t'} \mid L_t\right\}
\end{aligned}
\tag{4.2}
$$

According to Definition 1, the privacy-preserving method that satisfies Δ privacy can ensure that the amount of information contained in the published data in the edge node is less than $n\Delta$, where n is the number of sensitive locations. Users with strong privacy requirements at a given time can set Δ to 0. Therefore, users need to ensure that the published location data do not disclose the user's Δ privacy in any sensitive location; they only need to meet the $\frac{\Delta}{n}$ privacy.

4.1.2 Edge Nodes Clustering Scheme

As the first scheme in our DDSDP model, we approach edge node clustering to conceal the actual location information that the adversary might attack. This preserving scheme effectively prevents the adversary from intruding immediately and provides more complicated attack measurements. Each cluster contains at least two or more edge nodes to consist of a clustering approach. In the adversary attacking model, users are allocated into edge node clusters that cover more areas instead of direct connections. Necessary analyst steps are required for adversaries as precision selection becomes more challenged.

Unification Process and Weight Factors
Location based on distance measurement is one of the common location-aware privacy-preserving algorithms in edge computing. According to the user scenario, we analyze the time of arrival and the time difference of arrival to identify the distance. In the distance-based location algorithm, the user's location is usually calculated by each edge node. If the location information is leaked, the privacy

of users will be threatened. In addition, the designated edge node needs to know the location of each reference node to calculate the user's location. If the location information of the reference node is leaked, the adversary can launch location spoofing and other attacks on the reference node.

We created the location distance of designated edge nodes and first anchor node as matrix F, where the elements $F = F_1^1, F_2^1, F_3^1, F_\beta^1$ represent different factors of the same edge node and the elements $F = F_1^1, F_1^2, F_1^3, F_1^\alpha$ represent the same factor for different edge nodes. Thus, we express the matrix as

$$F = \begin{bmatrix} F_1^1 & F_2^1 & F_3^1 & \cdots & F_\beta^1 \\ F_1^2 & F_2^2 & F_3^2 & \cdots & F_\beta^2 \\ \cdots\cdots\cdots\cdots\cdots\cdots \\ F_1^\alpha & F_2^\alpha & F_3^\alpha & \cdots & F_\beta^\alpha \end{bmatrix} \tag{4.3}$$

According to the characteristics of edge nodes, they have different indices, such as access points and servers. A unification process is required to determine the distances before the aggregate indicator can be calculated. More specifically, the absolute values must be converted to relative values to solve the problem of different absolute values for different indices. The matrix F after the unification process is denoted by F'.

$$F' = \begin{bmatrix} \dfrac{F_1^1}{\sum_{i=1}^\alpha F_1^i} & \dfrac{F_2^1}{\sum_{i=1}^\alpha F_2^i} & \dfrac{F_3^1}{\sum_{i=1}^\alpha F_3^i} & \cdots & \dfrac{F_\beta^1}{\sum_{i=1}^\alpha F_\beta^i} \\[2ex] \dfrac{F_1^2}{\sum_{i=1}^\alpha F_1^i} & \dfrac{F_2^2}{\sum_{i=1}^\alpha F_2^i} & \dfrac{F_3^2}{\sum_{i=1}^\alpha F_3^i} & \cdots & \dfrac{F_\beta^2}{\sum_{i=1}^\alpha F_\beta^i} \\[2ex] \cdots\cdots\cdots\cdots\cdots\cdots\cdots\cdots\cdots \\[2ex] \dfrac{F_1^\alpha}{\sum_{i=1}^\alpha F_1^i} & \dfrac{F_2^\alpha}{\sum_{i=1}^\alpha F_2^i} & \dfrac{F_3^\alpha}{\sum_{i=1}^\alpha F_3^i} & \cdots & \dfrac{F_\beta^\alpha}{\sum_{i=1}^\alpha F_\beta^i} \end{bmatrix} \tag{4.4}$$

Cluster Triggering Process

Initially, all edge nodes are geographically allocated. We first introduce a cluster triggering approach when attacks have been identified by using the entropy weight method to allocate the measurements. The basic idea of the Entropy weight method (EWM) is to determine objective weights based on the variability of certain indicators. In our scenario, the EWM is applied to calculate the weight of each element in each dimension from the attacking model. Generally, a smaller elemental entropy e^j indicates that an element is more meaningful, providing more information and related to more data in the edge network, and thus should be assigned a greater weight in the associated dimension. In contrast, a larger entropy e^j indicates that an element is of smaller value, provides less information, and plays a smaller role in the overall evaluation, and thus, it should have a smaller weight.

Since the unification process has been applied, the weight factor must be calculated for each factor j in each dimension i, where $i = 1, 2 \ldots, n$ and $j = 1, 2 \ldots, m$.

$$p_{ij} = \frac{F'_{ij}}{\sum_{i=1}^{n} x_{ij}} \qquad (4.5)$$

Once the weight factors have been calculated, the entropy value of each factor j must be calculated, where $j = 1, 2 \ldots, m$. Here, $k = 1/\ln(n) > 0$ and $e_j >= 0$.

$$e_j = -k \sum_{i=1}^{n} p_{ij} \ln p_{ij} \qquad (4.6)$$

A redundancy rate is calculated to reduce the deviation during this process. For $j = 1, 2, \ldots, m$, the redundancy rate will be $d_j = 1 - e_j$. The weight factors after the redundancy correction are calculated as follows:

$$w_j = \frac{d_j}{\sum_{j=1}^{m} d_j} \qquad (4.7)$$

Since the weight factors for each element in each dimension have been determined, the clustering process is performed based on weight factors. Assume that t_{trig} is the threshold level for triggering clustering and depends on the distance of the edge network. T_{trig} is the result of the triggering process and depends on each element and its calculated weight factor. The clustering result depends on the edge node factor that is associated with the maximum value.

$$T_{trig}^1 = \frac{F_1^1}{\sum_{i=1}^{\alpha} F_1^i} \times t_{trig}$$

$$T_{trig}^2 = \frac{F_2^1}{\sum_{i=1}^{\alpha} F_2^i} \times t_{trig}$$

$$\ldots$$

$$T_{trig}^\beta = \frac{F_\beta^1}{\sum_{i=1}^{\alpha} F_\beta^i} \times t_{trig}$$

$$T_{trig} = max(T_{trig}^1, T_{trig}^2, \ldots, T_{trig}^\beta) \qquad (4.8)$$

4.2   System Analysis

We model a clustering model based on a modified affinity propagation (AP) mechanism. AP is a semi-supervised clustering algorithm based on nearest neighbor propagation that was proposed by Frey et al. [10]. Unlike in other clustering methods, in AP, it is not necessary to specify the final number of clusters. The cluster centers are selected from among the existing location data points instead of being generated as new data points. The model of the AP clustering method is less sensitive to the initial input location data and does not require the data similarity matrix to be symmetric. In an edge network, the input data can be of different types due to the different selections made by our triggering process based on the weight factors. Therefore, the AP algorithm is most suitable for clustering the edge nodes.

Preference
We first analyze the preference parameter. The clustering center similarity is defined as $sim(i, k)$, which represents the similarity between data point i and data point k. This similarity is calculated using the Euclidean distance:

$$sim(i, k) = \sqrt{\sum_{r=1}^{n}(i - k)^2 \times T_{trig}} \tag{4.9}$$

Responsibility
In the responsibility matrix, $r(i, k)$ denotes the extent to which data point k is suitable for being designated as the cluster center for data point i and represents a message sent from i to k, where $k \in 1, 2 \ldots, N$ and $k \neq k'$.

$$r(i, k) = (s(i, j) - max\{a(i, k') + sim(i, k')\}) \times T_{trig} \tag{4.10}$$

where $a(i, k')$ is a value representing the availability of point i to a point other than k, and its initial value is 0. $s(i, j)$ denotes the responsibility of points other than k to point i, where points outside of i are competing for the ownership of i. $r(i, k)$ denotes the cumulative responsibility of k to become the cluster center for i. When $r(i, k) > 0$, this indicates a greater responsibility of k to become the cluster center.

Availability
For the availability analysis, $a(i, k)$ denotes the likelihood that data point i will select data point k as its cluster center and represents a message sent from k to i.

$$a(i, k) = min\left\{0, r(k, k) + \sum_{k}\{max(0, r(i', k))\}\right\} \times T_{trig} \tag{4.11}$$

$$a(k, k) = (\sum_{k}\{max(0, r(i', k))\}) \times T_{trig} \tag{4.12}$$

where $r(i', k)$ denotes the responsibility value of point k as the cluster center for points other than i; all responsibility values that are greater than or equal to 0 are summed, and we also add the responsibility value of k as its own cluster center. Specifically, point k is supported by all data points with corresponding responsibility values greater than 0, and data point i selects k based on its cumulative value as a cluster center.

Damping Factor λ

As the algorithm iteratively updates the values of availability and responsibility, a damping factor is applied. The effect of this factor λ is to enable the AP algorithm to converge more efficiently. The damping factor takes on values between 0 and 1. During each iteration of the algorithm, λ acts on the responsibility and availability values to weight the update relative to the previous iteration.

$$r_n = (1 - \lambda) \times r_n + \lambda \times r_{n-1} \tag{4.13}$$

$$a_n = (1 - \lambda) \times a_n + \lambda \times a_{n-1} \tag{4.14}$$

4.3   Differential Privacy Protection Scheme

In edge computing, each user publishes their sensitive location data upon the connection created. However, this location information needs privacy protection before being published. We created the first scheme of clustering to increase the difficulty level when the adversary aims to attack. In addition, the model protects the released data with a customized protection level according to distances between clusters. Furthermore, our second scheme aims to provide ultimate privacy protection to users. Building upon the cluster modeling provided in the previous section, we compromised ϵ-differential privacy and added Laplacian noise into the cluster to obtain the ultimate protection.

QoS Data Utility Mapping

In the DDSDP model, we defined the distance between each cluster $sim(i, k)$ in the early paragraph, and we use the softmax function to model the QoS data utility function and privacy protection level ϵ. The softmax function assigns decimal probabilities to each class in a multi-class problem. It is also widely used to map the data utility and privacy protection level according to the QoS. The mapping function illustrated as

$$\text{QoS}(\epsilon_i) = k \times \frac{\exp(\theta_i^t sim_{ik} \cdot x)}{\sum_{k=1}^{K} \exp(\theta_k^t sim_{ik} \cdot x)} \tag{4.15}$$

where $k \in K$ is defined as the parameter to adjust the maximum amplitude value, θ is the steepness of the curve and x denotes the location.

Laplacian Mechanism and Laplacian Noise
We use probabilistic clustering on the original single clustering query results to protect location privacy. To protect users' location-aware content privacy, we use the Laplacian mechanism to change the real value by adding Laplacian noise to the original clustering result data so that the differential privacy is satisfied before and after adding noise.

$$M(D) = f(D) + Y$$

s.t.

$$Lap(\alpha) = \frac{p_x(z)}{p_y(z)} = exp(\frac{\epsilon \cdot \parallel f(x) - f(y) \parallel}{\triangle f})$$

(4.16)

where ϵ defines the privacy budget and ϵ can be customized due to the clustering requirement to achieve a better privacy budget result. Y determines the Laplacian distributed noise. $Lap(\alpha)$ defines the probability density of the mechanism, while α determines the size of the noise.

ϵ-Customizable Differential Privacy Formulation
After establishing QoS and Laplacian noise modeling, we model the ϵ-customized differential privacy mechanism, which provides the protection of data release in edge nodes. We use the distance calculation from the clustering mechanism and multihop with the QoS function to map the privacy protection level. In the edge computing clustering paradigm, users publish sensitive location data since connections occur. These data require protection to avoid being attacked by adversaries. In addition, edge nodes have different capacities and computational capabilities. Therefore, we develop the second scheme after the clustering mechanism as follows.

We use ϵ-customizable differential privacy to obtain our goal. We formulated the mechanism when $M \to \Delta(\chi)$ is considered to be ϵ-differentially privacy as

$$Pr[M(D) \in \Omega] = \exp(QoS(\epsilon_i)) \cdot Pr[M(D') \in \Omega]$$

$$= \exp(k \times \frac{\exp(\theta_i^t sim_{ik} \cdot x)}{\sum_{k=1}^{K} \exp(\theta_k^t sim_{ik} \cdot x)}) \cdot Pr[M(D') \in \Omega]$$

(4.17)

s.t.

$$\forall \Omega \subseteq \chi,$$

$$\forall (D, D') \subseteq \psi$$

where χ denotes the outcome of the noisy location and D defines the space of the sensitive location data, where $\epsilon \geq 0$, and $\psi \subseteq \forall (D, D') \subseteq \psi$ denotes the proximal relation between the data. We consider D_t and D_{t+1} as adjustable datasets to enable further dynamic features for the proposed model.

We define three qualifications to compromise the customizable privacy protection model and clustering model. The first qualification provides initial ϵ-customizable protection. We denote p_i as each piece of the sensitive location data, and $\epsilon(\frac{1}{d_{ik}})$ should be satisfied by approximations $\{y_{ik}\}$ from p_k. The purpose of the second qualification limits the composed privacy protection level for the upper bound edge node (source). For the maximum composition defined as

$$comp(\epsilon) = \sum_{i=1,k\neq 1}^{n} M_D(\epsilon(\frac{1}{d_{ik}})) \tag{4.18}$$

In the third qualification, we design the optimization of data utilities published by the user. The most accurate noise n from mechanism M should be the response of the actual output x_i. Furthermore, different approximations $\{y_{ik}\}$ lead to multiple values of data utility optimization. Thus, we express the sum of the data utility measurements as follows:

$$\sum_{i=1}^{n} \sum_{k\neq 1}^{n} E\| y_{ik} - x_i \|_2^2 \tag{4.19}$$

Therefore, optimized tradeoffs can be analyzed by a given maximum privacy protection level and minimum data utility that is expected.

$$\epsilon = k \times \frac{\exp(\theta_i^t sim_{ik} \cdot x)}{\sum_{k=1}^{K} \exp(\theta_k^t sim_{ik} \cdot x)}$$

$$\sum_{i=1,k\neq 1}^{n,n} M_D(\epsilon(\frac{1}{d_{ik}})) \leq max\, M_D(\epsilon(\frac{1}{d_{ik}})) \tag{4.20}$$

$$\sum_{i=1}^{n} \sum_{k\neq 1}^{n} E\| y_{ik} - x_i \|_2^2 \geq min(DU)$$

4.4   Performance Evaluation

In this section, we run a series of simulations to test the performance of our proposed DDSDP model in several ways. First, we evaluate the data utilities by sampling time slots with different locations; then, we evaluate privacy protection levels with different time slots by different locations. The third part of the experiment evaluates the performance of the clustering approach, including clustering results, transmission results, clustering distance, and loading performance for the overall edge nodes. To verify these results, we use the latest version of the VicFreeWiFi Access Point Locations dataset [11], which contains 571 raw location information data points. This dataset is available in several locations across 300 km and allows 250 MB per device per day. The dataset contains detailed location information for the access points, including 391 nodes recorded in the city center, 44 nodes in the northbound area, and 82 nodes in the west-northbound area. This location information leads to location-aware issues for adversaries in determining users.

In the following experiments, we first evaluate the performance of the clustering efficiency, as SDN-enabled edge computing should contain more customization features without affecting the original performance. The SDN-enabled clustering results demonstrate better network performance. Then, we analyze our DDSDP model with different ϵ values to obtain the best performance and customization of the ϵ-differential privacy protection scheme. Moreover, we also compare our DDSDP model with two other mechanisms: classic ϵ-differential privacy (CDP) and classic customizable differential privacy (CCDP) against attacking formulations. CDPs have fixed circumstances and generate noise from the Laplacian mechanism. The CCDP has a customizable privacy level and complies with noise from the Laplacian mechanism.

4.4.1 Clustering Analysis

Figure 4.2 shows the node clustering results generated via the first scheme clustering method from our DDSDP model. In these results, the estimated number of clusters is 16, and these clusters are formed from 517 available edge nodes. We test three

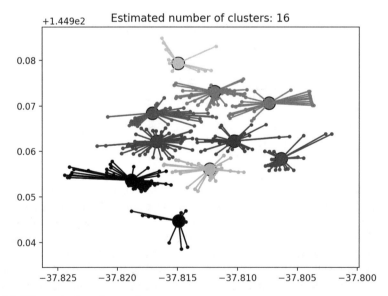

Fig. 4.2 Edge node clustering results

similarity values to evaluate system performance. Among the results, the minimum similarity is $2.000000e^{-8}$, and the median and maximum similarity values are 0.017874 and 1.276488, respectively. The similarity is based on the longitudinal and latitudinal locations along with the connection speed. The homogeneity rate is 0.513, which indicates the extent to which nodes with the same properties are clustered. In this particular dataset, the rate is based predominantly on the connection speed. The completeness and V-measure results are 0.133 and 0.211, respectively, and the adjusted Rand index is 0.080. The clustering results are generated by the first scheme clustering system, resulting in a good performance.

4.4.2 Data Utilities Performance

Figure 4.3 shows the results of the data utilities according to our DSDP model. This figure demonstrates the general trends of the QoS functionality. We select three customized representative parameter values for the ϵ, which when $\epsilon = 1$, $\epsilon = 0.5$, and $\epsilon = 0.1$, by comparing with raw data value to observe our results, which makes it applicable to various scenarios. We start with the clustering algorithm to choose 20 available clustered edge networks, which are clustered networks based on QoS measurements from the clustering distances. The Laplacian mechanism is responsible for generating noisy responses. As shown in the figure, smaller ϵ values

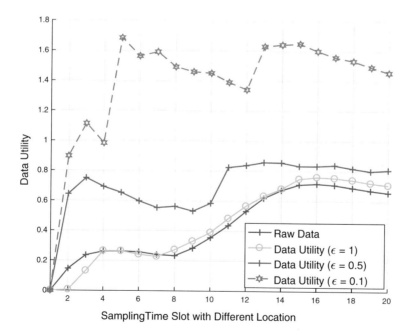

Fig. 4.3 Data utilities performance among three ϵ values

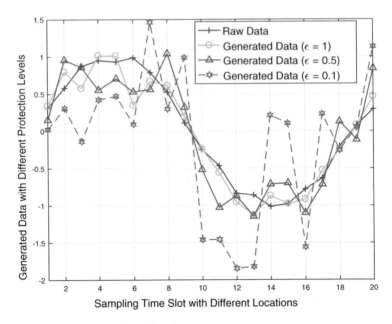

Fig. 4.4 Privacy levels with different locations

lead to better overall data utility performance values. For the particular dataset scenarios, when the ϵ value equals 0.1, we achieve the peak value, which is 1.7 with clustering time slot 5.

Furthermore, we consider different clustering situations in terms of the performance for the privacy protection level. In the initialization stage, we enable three representative parameter values that are the same as the data utilities evaluation to set up the customized ϵ. The reason to choose three ϵ values is to simulate the randomness of the Laplacian mechanism, which leads to different noisy responses. As shown in Fig. 4.4, privacy protection level comparison in terms of customizable ϵ is based on cluster distance. Sampling time slot 7 with one of the clusters reaches the maximum privacy protection level of 1.5, and the cluster in time slot 20 remains at the highest value along with the other three values. Although the performance for three parameters obtains different results from different clusters, it justifies the outstanding importance of customization. For example, for time slot 4's cluster, we customize the ϵ value to 1.

4.4.3 Performances Against Attacking Models

Figures 4.5 and 4.6 demonstrate the performance evaluation in the wormhole attacking scenario for the privacy protection level against both individual and clustered edge nodes. A comprehensive comparison result between the DDSDP

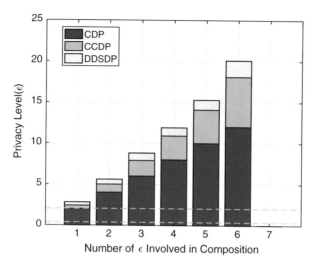

Fig. 4.5 Attacking scenario 1: multiple users share location data to individual edge node

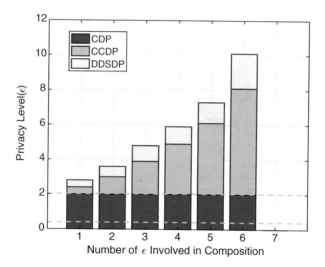

Fig. 4.6 Attacking scenario 1: multiple users share location data to clustered edge nodes

model and the other two classic models: CDP and CCDP are presented in the same histogram. In addition, two dotted green lines demonstrate the ϵ value of the data that the adversary has. As shown in the results, a smaller ϵ leads to a better privacy protection level. Since we use ϵ-differential privacy to accomplish our model, we observe that a smaller value of ϵ demonstrates fewer data that are provided to the adversaries. We set two values of ϵ. When ($\epsilon = 0.45$) represents that the adversary can determine most of the data from the location and knowledgeable for most of the attacking models. The upper dotted green line represents the ($\epsilon = 2.05$), where CDP and CCDP are fully functional and can provide comprehensive protection for users. However, for all the ϵ values between the dotted green lines, only our proposed DDSDP model can achieve the optimal protection goal. Therefore, we can conclude that DDSDP can provide better protection schemes when the attacks occur where CDP and CCDP struggle for different scenarios.

Figures 4.7 and 4.8 both demonstrate the performance for our proposed DDSDP model where the attacking scenario is a DDoS attack. We use both ϵ values from previous figures where ($\epsilon = 0.45$) and ($\epsilon = 2.05$). As shown from the results, CDP

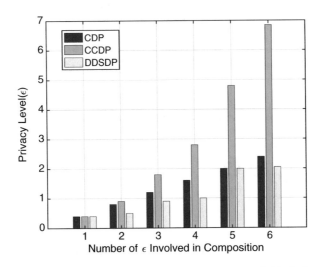

Fig. 4.7 Attacking scenario 2: multiple users share location data to individual edge node

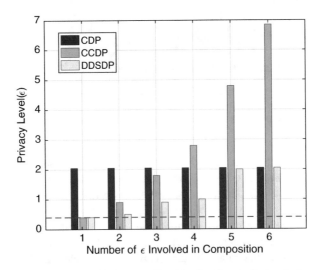

Fig. 4.8 Attacking scenario 2: multiple users share location data to clustered edge node

is unaffected against the DDoS attacking scenario since the composition mechanism is still free. In addition, for DDSDP and CCDP, the privacy protection levels increase while the ϵ increases from 0.45. However, DDSDP demonstrates that no further information will be gathered by two or more adversaries after an attack. The sum of the ϵ value equals the maximum ϵ value when attack occurred. Therefore, the DDSDP model we proposed above demonstrates better performances in terms of both popular attacking methods.

4.5 Summary

In this chapter, we proposed an integrated privacy protection model (DDSD) in the SDN-enabled edge computing paradigm. According to two popular attacking methods, our proposed model provides dual-scheme protection approaches, including edge node clustering and ϵ-customizable differential privacy. We first formulated the attacking model as the preliminary work and then developed our first clustering-based protection scheme. The first scheme adds multiple nodes in one cluster so that adversaries cannot determine the location data in the first place. We then developed our second protection scheme with a ϵ-customizable differential privacy approach. Laplacian noise was added into the cluster. The extensive experimental results demonstrated that the proposed model and clustering algorithm not only provides considerable reliability in designated scenarios but also constitutes customizable location-aware data privacy protection.

References

1. C. Mouradian, D. Naboulsi, S. Yangui, R.H. Glitho, M.J. Morrow, P.A. Polakos, A comprehensive survey on fog computing: state-of-the-art and research challenges. IEEE Commun. Surv. Tutor. **20**(1), 416–464 (2018)
2. M. Yannuzzi, R. Milito, R. Serral-Graciá, D. Montero, M. Nemirovsky, Key ingredients in an iot recipe: fog computing, cloud computing, and more fog computing, in *2014 IEEE 19th International Workshop on Computer Aided Modeling and Design of Communication Links and Networks (CAMAD)* (2014), pp. 325–329
3. J. Ni, K. Zhang, X. Lin, X. Shen, Securing fog computing for internet of things applications: challenges and solutions. IEEE Commun. Surv. Tutor. **20**(1), 601–628 (2018)
4. B. Gu, X. Wang, Y. Qu, J. Jin, Y. Xiang, L. Gao, Context-aware privacy preservation in a hierarchical fog computing system, in *ICC 2019 - 2019 IEEE International Conference on Communications (ICC)* (2019), pp. 1–6
5. J. Zhang, X. Feng, Z. Liu, A grid-based clustering algorithm via load analysis for industrial internet of things. IEEE Access **PP**, 1–1 (2018)
6. H. Kim, E.A. Lee, S. Dustdar, Creating a resilient IoT with edge computing. Computer **52**(8), 43–53 (2019)
7. G. Potrino, F. De Rango, P. Fazio, A distributed mitigation strategy against DoS attacks in edge computing, in *2019 Wireless Telecommunications Symposium (WTS)* (2019), pp. 1–7

8. Y. Xiao, Y. Jia, C. Liu, X. Cheng, J. Yu, W. Lv, Edge computing security: state of the art and challenges. Proc. IEEE **107**(8), 1608–1631 (2019)
9. Deepali, K. Bhushan, DDoS attack defense framework for cloud using fog computing, in *2017 2nd IEEE International Conference on Recent Trends in Electronics, Information Communication Technology (RTEICT)* (2017), pp. 534–538
10. B.J. Frey, D. Dueck, Clustering by passing messages between data points. Science **315**(5814), 972–976 (2007)
11. VicFreeWiFi Access Point locations, Discover.data.vic.gov.au (2017). [Online]. Available: https://discover.data.vic.gov.au/dataset/2f2b954a-ee69-493e-8071-0754d01fd11f/ resource/1922597e-c989-4ebd-bec9-afcc284e5b2c/download/vicfreewifi20ap20map20data 2020170724.csv [Accessed: 20- Sept-2018]

Chapter 5
Blockchain Based Decentralized Privacy Preserving in Edge Computing

Despite the provided conveniences, privacy issues are emerging because data sharing is trending to improve the service performances. It is essential for end devices to share local data to central authorities such as edge servers for global aggregation [1]. The uploaded data usually contains some unique identifiers, location information, and trajectories, which may lead to further privacy leakage or potential financial loss [2, 3]. On the other side, privacy protection should not dramatically degrade data utility [4]. Otherwise, the optimization and prediction results will be misled by the inaccurate global aggregation results, which invalidates the advanced services of edge computing.

In addition, the communication cost keeps increasing in this big data era. If certain privacy protection mechanisms are deployed, more communication resources will be occupied, which will be another bottleneck of edge computing [5, 6]. In this scenario, there is a high demand on real-time communication as network traffic flow undergoes a myriad of instant changes [7].

To address the aforementioned issues, some existing works have made attempts from different angles. Classic privacy protection framework, differential privacy [8] with its extensions [9], is leveraged to deal with the aggregation privacy [10]. However, it is difficult to find a universal optimal tradeoff between data utility and privacy protection [4]. Encryption-based methods, such as the work conducted in [11], can preserve privacy in a satisfying degree but is not scalable to big data scenarios. Federated learning [12], which is a new-merging technology, can achieve efficiency communication by exchanging updates between local models and global models [13]. But another concern arises that the central authority may be compromised and poisoning attacks are launched by adversaries. Blockchain is introduced to this scenario to eliminate the trust issues here [14]. But strictly providing privacy protection only on blockchain and efficiency encumber the feasibility of direct applications.

Motivated by this, we introduce a blockchain-enabled federated learning (FL-Block) model by replacing the central authority with a specially designed blockchain with decentralized privacy protocols. In FL-Block, end devices will upload the local updates to the edge servers, where the global updates will be generated and stored. Since only the pointer of the global updates is saved on-chain while a distributed hash table (DHT) is used to save the data, the block generation efficiency could be guaranteed. With a hybrid identity generation, comprehensive verification, access control, and off-chain data storage and retrieve, FL-Block enables decentralized privacy protection while preventing single point failure. Moreover, the poisoning attack could be eliminated from the side of edge servers.

The novelty of this chapter is summarized as follows.

- **Decentralized Privacy:** By integrating blockchain with federated learning, FL-Block enables decentralized privacy protection and prevents single point failure in edge computing scenario. In addition, blockchain could provide incentives to federated learning participants.
- **Poisoning Attack Proof:** Poisoning attacks can be eliminated because central authority is replaced by a novel blockchain system which provides non-tempering feature. The protection mechanism is further enhanced due to the elimination of poisoning attacks.
- **High Efficiency:** Two important characteristics jointly contribute to high efficiency. The first one is federated learning that only requires the exchange of training updates. The other one is only the pointer which saved on blockchain while the associated data is saved in an off-chain distributed hash table.

5.1 System Modeling

In this section, we present the architecture of the blockchain-enabled federated learning (FL-Block). We use v_i and m_j to denote different end devices and miners, respectively. Then ds_k is used to present different data samples. In addition, we use e_l to differentiate the global model update iterations, which is also referred to as epochs.

5.1.1 Federated Learning in FL-Block

In FL-Block, the federated learning is achieved by a cluster of end devices $V = \{1, 2, \ldots, N_V \in V\}$ where $|V| = N_V$. The i-th device V_i possesses a set of data samples DS_i where $|DS_i| = N_i$. V_i trains its local data and the local model updates of the device V_i are uploaded to its associated miner M_i instead of a trusted third party. The miner M_i is selected from a set of miners $M = \{1, 2, \ldots, N_M\}$ randomly, where $|M| = N_M$. $M = V$ could be satisfied when the miners M_i are physically identical to the end devices. Otherwise, we will have $M \neq DS$. Moving on, the total number of v_i of the local model updates are verified and shared among all possible miners. Finally, the aggregated global model updates are downloaded from each miner to its corresponding device.

To further improve, the decentralized model training concentrates on solving a linear regression problem on a series of parallel data samples $DS = \cup_{i=1}^{N_V} DS_i$ where $|DS| = N_S$. The k-th data sample $ds_k \in DS$ is given as $s_k = \{x_k, y_k\}$ for a d-dimensional column vector $x_k \in R^d$ as well as a scalar value $y_k \in R$. The objective of the linear regression problem is to minimize a pre-defined loss function $f(\omega)$ with respect to a d-dimensional column vector $\omega \in R^d$, which is regarded as a global weight. To simplify this process, the pre-defined loss function $f(\omega)$ is selected as the mean squared error (MSE) in the following context.

$$f(\omega) = \frac{1}{N_D S} \sum_{i=1}^{N_V} \sum_{s_k \in S_i} f_k(\omega) \tag{5.1}$$

where $f_k(\omega)(x_k^T \omega - y_k)^2/2$ and the notation $(.)^T$ denotes the vector transpose operation. This could be easily extended to various loss functions under diverse neural network models with minor operations.

For purpose of solving the aforementioned issues, the learning model of the end device V_i is trained locally with the data sample set DS_i using a stochastic variance reduced gradient (SVRG) algorithm, and all local model updates of the devices are aggregated using a distributed approximate Newton (DANE) method, which will be trained to generate the global model update.

To further improve this model, the ceiling of the global model is set to L epochs. For each epoch, the local model of end device V_i is updated with the number N_i of iterations. Therefore, we can have the local weight $\omega_i^{(t,l)} \in R^d$ of the end device V_i at the $t_t h$ local iteration of the l-th epoch as

$$\omega_i^{(t,l)} = \omega_i^{(t-1,l)}$$
$$- \frac{\beta}{N_i} \left\{ \left[\nabla f_k(\omega_i^{(t-1,l)}) - \nabla f_k(\omega^{(l)}) \right] + \nabla f(\omega^{(l)}) \right\} \tag{5.2}$$

where $\beta > 0$ is defined as a step size, $\omega^{(l)}$ is the global weight at the l-th epoch, and $\nabla f(\omega^{(l)}) = 1/N_{DS} \cdot \sum_{i=1}^{N_V} \sum_{s_k \in S_i} \nabla f_k(\omega^{(l)})$ is derived from Eq. 5.1. We use $\omega^{(l)}$ to represent the local weight when the last local iteration of the l-th epoch is finished, i.e., $\omega_i^{(l)} = \omega_i^{(N_i,l)}$. Built upon this, the update of the global weight $\omega^{(l)}$ is formulated as

$$\omega^{(l)} = \omega^{(l-1)} + \sum_{i=1}^{N_V} \frac{N_i}{N_{DS}} \left(\omega_i^{(l)} - \omega_i^{(l-1)} \right) \tag{5.3}$$

The iteration process of updating the local and global weights will continue until the constraint of global weight $\omega^{(l)}$ satisfies $|\omega^{(L)} - \omega^{(L-1)}| \leq \epsilon$ is satisfies, where $\epsilon > 0$ is a small positive constant.

In the classic federated learning settings, at the l-th epoch, the end device V_i is supposed to upload its local model update $\left(\omega_i^{(l)}, \{\nabla f_k(\omega^{(l)})\}_{s_k \in S_i}\right)$ to the edge servers, with the model update size δ_m that is identically specified for each end device. The global model updates $\left(\omega^{(l)}, \nabla f(\omega^{(l)})\right)$ with the same size δ_m are computed by the edge servers, which will be downloaded to all end devices after processing. In FL-Block, the edge server entity is substituted with a blockchain network which is discussed in detail in the following subsection.

5.1.2   Blockchain in FL-Block

Regarding the blockchain network settings of FL-Block, the generated blocks and the cross verification by the miners M are devised to upload truthful data of the local model updates. This is achieved by developing a specially designed distributed ledger. The protocols of the distributed ledger are discussed in the next section in detail. Each block in the distributed ledger contains body and header sectors. In the classic blockchain structure, the body sector usually contains a set of verified transactions. In FL-Block, the body stores the local model updates of the devices in V, i.e., $\left(\omega_i^{(l)}, \{\nabla f_k(\omega^{(l)})\}_{s_k \in S_i}\right)$ for the device V_i at the l-th epoch, as well as its local computation time $T_{\{local,i\}}^{(l)}$. Extended from the classic blockchain structure, the header sector stores the information of a pointer to the previous block, block generation rate λ, and the output value of the consensus algorithm, namely the nonce. In this context, the proof of work (PoW) is used as the instance consensus algorithm, while all other consensus algorithms can be extended into this scenario. In order to store the local model updates of all the end devices, the size of each block is defined as $h + \delta_m N_V$, where h and δ_m denote the header size and model update size, respectively.

Each miner is assigned with a candidate block that contains local model updates information from its binding end devices or other miners, in the order of arrival. The writing procedure will continue until the block size is fully filled or a maximum waiting time T_{wait} is reached from the beginning of each epoch. To make it simplified, we use a sufficiently long T_{wait} so that every block is filled with local model updates of all end devices.

In the next stage, the miner keeps generating a random nonce until it becomes smaller than a target value using PoW. Once one of the miners M_1 works out the nonce, its corresponding candidate block is allowed to be generated as a new block. Intuitively, the block generation rate λ can be carefully controlled by modifying the difficulty of the deployed PoW consensus algorithm.

Furthermore, the newly generated block is shared to all other miners for the purpose of synchronizing all existing distributed ledgers. To achieve this, all the other miners who received the newly generated block are enforced to quit the calculation process. Then, the generated block is linked to the local ledgers maintained by the miners. However, there is a possibility of forking when another miner M_2 happens to generate a candidate block within the sharing delay of the eligible block. Some miners may falsely link the ineligible block to their local ledgers. In FL-Block, forking will mislead the end devices linking the ineligible block to train a poisoned global update and subsequently generate offtrack local updates in the next iteration.

The value of forking frequency is positively correlated with both the blockchain generate rate λ and the block sharing delay. The mitigation of forking will lead to an extra delay, which will be discussed in Sect. 5.2.

Apart from the above operation for local model updates uploading, the blockchain also provides proper rewards for data samples to the end devices and for the verification operation to the miners, which is referred to as data reward and mining reward, respectively. The data reward of the end devices V_i is received from its corresponding miner, and the amount of the reward is linearly proportional to the size of the data sample N_i. After a block is generated by the miner M_j, the mining reward is earned from the blockchain network. Similarly, the amount of mining reward is linearly proportional to the aggregated data sample size of its all binding end devices, namely $\sum_{i=1}^{N_{M_j}}$, where N_{M_j} denotes the number of end devices binding with the miner M_j. This will provide the incentive to the miners so that they will process more local model updates while compensating their expenditure for the data reward.

However, there is a side effect in this rewarding system. There might be malicious end devices deceiving the miners by poisoning their actual sample sizes. In this case, the miners are supposed to verify eligible local updates before storing the local model updates in their associated candidate blocks. In this context, the simplified verification operation is conducted by comparing the sample size N_i with its corresponding computation time $T_{\{local,i\}}^{(}l)$ that is assumed to be reliable, following the proof of elapsed time under Intel's SGX technology.

As shown in Fig. 5.1, the FL-Block operation of the end device V_i at the l-th epoch can be explained by eight procedures as follows.

In the initialization part ($l = 1$), the initial parameters are uniformly randomly chosen from pre-defined ranges of the local and global weights $\{\omega_i^{(0)}, \omega^{(0)} \in (0, \omega_{max}]\}$ for a constant ω_{max}, and the global gradient $\nabla f(\omega^{(0)}) \in (0, 1]$.

In local model update phase, the end device V_i computes Eq. 5.2 with the number N_i of iterations.

In local model upload phase, the end device V_i uniformly randomly associates with the miner M_i. If $M = V$, miner M_i is selected from M V_i. The end device uploads the local model updates $\left(\omega_i^{(l)}, \{\nabla f_k(\omega^{(l)})\}_{s_k \in S_i}\right)$ and the corresponding local computation time $T_{\{local,i\}}^{(l)}$ to the associated miner.

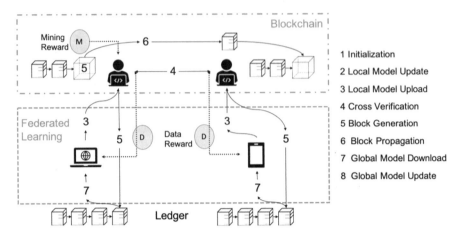

Fig. 5.1 Blockchain-enabled federated learning diagram

Algorithm 2 Block-enabled federated learning algorithm

Input: End devices V_i, Edge servers, Miners M_i;
Output: Optimized Global Model;
 1: Initialization;
 2: **while** New data sample DS is generated **do**
 3:     Local model update by V_i;
 4:     Local model upload to edge servers;
 5:     Cross verification by M_i;
 6:     Block generation by the winning miner;
 7:     **if** M_i finds the nonce of the new block b_i **then**
 8:         Link b_i to the blockchain
 9:         Remove all other relevant blocks $\hat{b}_i$;
10:     **end if**
11:     Block propagation;
12:     Global model update by edge servers;
13:     Global model download to V_i;
14: **end while**
15: Output the eligible global model.

In cross-verification phase, the miners broadcast the local model updates obtained from their associated end devices. At the same time, the miners verify the received local model updates from their associated devices or the other miners in the order of arrival. The truthfulness of the local model updates is validated, if the local computation time $T_{\{local,i\}}^{(l)}$ is proportional to the data sample size N_i. The verified local model updates are recorded in the miner's candidate block, until it is reaching the block size $(h + \delta_m N_V)$ or the maximum waiting time T_{wait}.

In block generation phase, each miner starts running the PoW until either it finds the nonce or it receives a generated block from another miner.

In the block propagation phase, denoting as $M_{\hat{o}} \in M$ the miner who first finds the nonce. Its candidate block is generated as a new block that is broadcasted to all miners. In order to avoid forking, an acknowledgment (ACK) signal is transmitted when each miner detects no forking event. Each miner waits until receiving ACK signals of all miners. Otherwise, the operation goes back and iterates from phase 2.

In global model download phase, the end device V_i downloads the generated block from its associated miner M_i.

In global model update phase, the end device V_i locally computes the global model update in Eq. 5.3 by using the aggregate local model updates stored in the generated block.

The one-epoch procedure continues until the global weight $\omega^{(L)}$ satisfies $\omega^{(L)} - \omega^{(L-1)} \leq \epsilon$. The centralized FL structure is vulnerable to the malfunction of edge server, which distorts the global model updates of all end devices. Compared to this, each end device in FL-Block locally computes its global model update, which is thus more robust to the malfunction of the miners that replace the edge server entity.

5.2   System Analysis

In this section, we first analyze poisoning attacks. Then, we consider a reference end device $V_o \in V$ that is randomly selected. The objective is to derive the optimal block generation rate $\lambda*$, which minimizes the learning completion latency T_o. In this work, we define T_o as the total elapsed time during L epochs at the end device V_o. This latency is linearly proportional to the l-th epoch latency, i.e., $T_o = \sum_{l=1}^{L} T_o^{(l)}$. Thus, we hereafter focus only on $T_o^{(l)}$ without loss of generality.

5.2.1   Poisoning Attacks and Defense

Beyond the naive approach that an adversary trains the local model based on specially designed falsified data, the enhanced attack is referred as model substitution, in which the adversary tries to replace the global model GM^{t+1} with a malicious model MM, which is shown in Eq. 5.4.

$$G_{t+1} = GM^t + \frac{r}{n} \sum_{j=1}^{m} \left(LM_j^{t+1} - GM^t \right)$$

$$\Rightarrow MM = GM^t + \frac{r}{n} \sum_{j=1}^{m} \left(LM_j^{t+1} - GM^t \right)$$

(5.4)

in which t is the current time slot, r is the learning rate, LM is a local model, n is number the total edge devices, and m is the number participants.

Since non-IID data is used in this case, each local model may be quite different from the global model. With the convergence of the global model, the deviations cancel out bit by bit, which can be denoted as $\sum_{j=1}^{m-1}(LM_j^{t+1} - GM^t) \rightarrow 0$. Based on this, an adversary may upload a model as

$$\widetilde{LM_m^{t+1}} = \frac{n}{r}MM - \left(\frac{n}{r} - 1\right)GM^t - \sum_{j=1}^{m-1}\left(LM_j^{t+1} - GM^t\right)$$

$$\simeq \frac{n}{r}\left(MM - GM^t\right) + GM^t \tag{5.5}$$

This enhanced attack increases the weights of the malicious model MM by $\eta = n/r$ to guarantee the replacement of the global model GM by MM. This attack functions better when the convergence is nearly reached. In addition, if the adversary is blind to the value of n and r, he/she can simply increase the value of η in every iteration. Although scaling by $\eta \leq n/r$ only partially replaces the GM, the attack still functions well.

5.2.2 Single-Epoch FL-Block Latency Model

Following the FL-Block operation in Sect. 5.1.2, the end device $V_o's$ l-th epoch latency $T_o^{(l)}$ is not only determined by communication and block generation delays but also determined by the computation cost by federated learning (Fig. 5.2).

To begin with, the computation costs are caused by phase 2 and phase 8 defined in Sect. 5.1.2. Let δ_d denote the size of a single data sample that is given identically for all data samples. δ_d/f_c is required to process δ_d with the clock speed f_C. We formulate $T_{\{local,i\}}^{(l)}$ (local model updating delay) in phase 2 as $T_{\{local,i\}}^{(l)} = \delta_d N_o/f_c$. Analogically, we define the global model updating delay $T_{\{global,o\}}^{(l)}$ in phase 8 as $T_{\{global,o\}}^{(l)} = \delta_m N_V/f_c$.

Then, we discuss the communication delays existed in phase 3 and phase 7 between the miners and corresponding end devices. With additive white Gaussian noise (AWGN) channels, we evaluate the achievable rate using Shannon capacity. In term of phase 3, the local model uploading delay $T_{\{up,o\}}^{(l)}$ is formulated as $T_{\{up,o\}}^{(l)} = \delta_m/\left[W_{up}\log_2(1 + \lambda_{\{up,o\}})\right]$, where W_{up} is known as the uplink bandwidth allocation for each end device while $\lambda_{\{up,o\}}$ is the received signal-to-noise ratio (SNR) of miner M_o. Similarly, in phase 7, we define the communication delay of global model. The downloading delay $T_{\{vn,o\}}^{(l)}$ is described as $T_{\{vn,o\}}^{(l)} = h + \delta_m N_V/\left[W_{dn}\log_2(1 + \lambda_{\{dn,o\}})\right]$, where W_{dn} is the downlink bandwidth allocation for each device and $\lambda_{\{dn,o\}}$ is the received signal-to-noise ratio of device V_o.

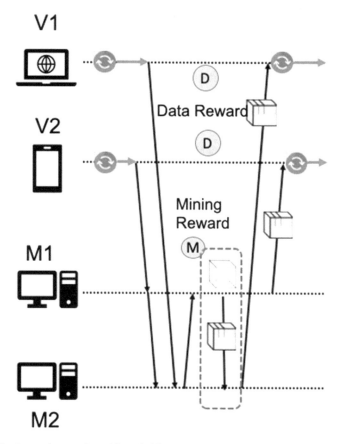

Fig. 5.2 Single-epoch operation without forking

In addition, the communication delay also exists when miners are communicating in the blockchain network, which is part of phase 4 and phase 5. Since the cross-verification time is insignificant compared with the communication costs, the cross-verification delay $T^{(l)}_{\{cross,o\}}$ in phase 4 is defined under frequency division multiple access (FDMA) as

$$T^{(l)}_{\{cross,o\}} = \max\left\{ T_{wait} - \left(T^{(l)}_{\{local,i\}} + T^{(l)}_{\{up,o\}} \right), \right.$$

$$\left. \sum_{M_j \in M \setminus M_o} \delta_m N_{M_j} / \left[W_m \log_2(1 + \lambda_{oj}) \right] \right\} \tag{5.6}$$

where we use W_m to denote the bandwidth allocation per each miner link and λ_{oj} is the received SNR from the miner M_o to the miner M_j. Similarly, $M_{\hat{o}} \in M$ is regarded as the miner who first finds the nonce. Then, the total block propagation delay $T_{\{bp,\hat{o}\}}^{(l)}$ in phase 6 is formulated as $T_{\{bp,\hat{o}\}}^{(l)} = \max_{M_j \in M \setminus M_{\hat{o}}} \left\{ t_{\{bp,j\}}^{(l)} \right\}$ under frequency division multiple access. The term $\left\{ t_{\{bp,j\}}^{(l)} \right\} = (h = \delta_m N_V) / \left[W_m \log_2(1 + \lambda_{\hat{o}j}) \right]$ represents the block sharing delay from the mining winner $M_{\hat{o}}$ to $M_j \in M \setminus M_{\hat{o}}$, and $\lambda_{\hat{o}j}$ is received SNR from the miner $M_{\hat{o}}$ to the miner M_j.

The last considered delay is the block generation delay in phase 5. The miner $M_j \in M$'s block generation delay $T_{\{bg,j\}}^{(l)}$ complies with an exponential distribution with a mean value of $1/\lambda$. The block generation delay $T_{\{bg,\hat{o}\}}^{(l)}$ of the mining winner $M_{\hat{o}}$ is given as the delay of interest. Based on this, the latency $T_o^{(L)}$ of the l-th epoch is described as

$$
T_o^{(l)} = N_{folk}^{(l)} \left(T_{\{local,o\}}^{(l)} + T_{\{up,o\}}^{(l)} + T_{\{cross,o\}}^{(l)} + T_{\{bg,\hat{o}\}}^{(l)} \right. \\
\left. + T_{\{bp,\hat{o}\}}^{(l)} \right) + T_{\{vn,o\}}^{(l)} + T_{\{global,o\}}^{(l)}
\tag{5.7}
$$

in which the $N_{folk}^{(l)}$ represents forking occurrences' number in the l-th epoch. The forking occurrences comply with a geometric distribution where mean is $1/(1 - p_{folk}^{(l)})$ and the forking probability is $p_{folk}^{(l)}$. Extended from phase 6, the forking probability is defined as

$$
p_{folk}^{(l)} = 1 - \prod_{M_j \in M \setminus M_{\hat{o}}} \Pr\left(t_j^{(l)} - t_{\hat{o}}^{(l)} > t_{bp,j}^{(l)} \right)
\tag{5.8}
$$

where the term $t_j^{(l)} = T_{\{local,j\}}^{(l)} + T_{\{up,j\}}^{(l)} + T_{\{cross,j\}}^{(l)} + T_{\{bg,j\}}^{(l)}$ is the cumulated delay until the miner M_j generates a block.

5.2.3   Optimal Generation Rate of Blocks

In this work, we target on deriving the optimal block generation rate λ^*, which can minimize the latency averaged over the consensus algorithm of the end device V_O's l-th epoch by means of the single-epoch latency expression in Eq. 5.7. The consensus process has an impact on three indexes, including the block sharing delay $T_{\{bp,\hat{o}\}}^{(l)}$, the block generation delay $T_{\{bg,\hat{o}\}}^{(l)}$, and the number $N_{folk}^{(l)}$ fork of forking occurrences (Fig. 5.3). These three entities are inter-dependent because of the existence of mining winner M_O. Solving this requires to compare the cumulated delays for all miners and their associated end devices edge server under their asynchronous operations that complicate the optimization.

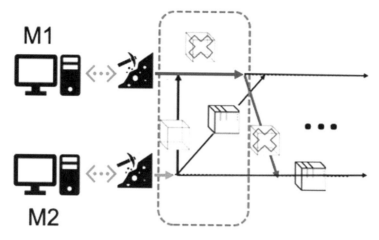

Fig. 5.3 Single-epoch operation with forking

To eliminate the above-mentioned difficulty, all miners are considered to start their consensus processes synchronously by modifying T_{wait}, with which we further derive $T_{\{cross,o\}}^{(l)} = T_{wait} - (T_{\{local,o\}}^{(l)} + T_{\{up,o\}}^{(l)})$. Under these circumstances, if the miners complete the cross-verification phase earlier, they are supposed to wait until T_{wait}, which provides lower bound of the performance, for instance, latency upper bound. Through exact operations using the synchronous approximation, the optimal block generation rate λ^* could be derived in a closed-form as follows.

Proposition 1 *With the PoW synchronous approximation, such as* $T_{\{cross,o\}}^{(l)} = T_{wait} - (T_{\{local,o\}}^{(l)} + T_{\{up,o\}}^{(l)})$, *the block generation rate* λ^* *minimizing the l-th epoch latency* $E[t_o^{(l)}]$ *averaged over the PoW process is given by*

$$\lambda^* \approx 2 \times \left(T_{\{bp,\hat{o}\}}^{(l)} \left[1 + \sqrt{1 + 4N_M \times \left(1 + T_{wait}/T_{\{bp,\hat{o}\}}^{(l)} \right)} \right] \right) \tag{5.9}$$

Next, we apply both the mean $1/(1 - p_{folk}^{(l)})$ of the geometrically distributed $N_{folk}^{(l)}$ and the synchronous consensus approximation to Eq. 5.7 and thus have

$$E[t_o^{(l)}] \approx \left(T_{wait} + E[T_{\{bg,\hat{o}\}}^{(l)}] \right) \Big/ \left(1/(1 - p_{folk}^{(l)}) \right) \\ + T_{\{vn,o\}}^{(l)} + T_{\{global,o\}}^{(l)} \tag{5.10}$$

There are some constant delays, including T_{wait}, $T_{\{vn,o\}}^{(l)}$, and $T_{\{global,o\}}^{(l)}$, which are given in Sect. 5.1.1. Based on these, we further derive the remainder as below.

For the probability $p_{folk}^{(l)}$, using Eq. 5.8 with $t_j^{(l)} - t_{\hat{o}}^{(l)} = t_{\{bg,j\}}^{(l)} - t_{\{bg,\hat{o}\}}^{(l)}$ under the synchronous approximation, we obtain the fork as

$$p_{folk}^{(l)} = 1 - \mathrm{EXP}\left(\lambda \sum_{M_j \in M \backslash M_{\hat{o}}} T_{\{bp,j\}}^{(l)}\right) \tag{5.11}$$

where $T_{\{bp,j\}}^{(l)}$ is a given constant delay. Then, by jointly using $T_{\{bg,\hat{o}\}}^{(l)}$ and the complementary cumulative distribution function (CCDF) of $T_{\{bg,j\}}^{(l)}$ which is the exponentially distributed, CCDF of $T_{\{bg,\hat{o}\}}^{(l)}$ is formulated as

$$\Pr\left(T_{\{bg,\hat{o}\}}^{(l)} > x\right) = \prod_{j=1}^{N_M} \Pr\left(T_{\{bg,j\}}^{(l)} > x\right) = \mathrm{EXP}\left(-\lambda N_M x\right) \tag{5.12}$$

Moreover, we apply the total probability theorem, which yields $E[T_{\{bg,\hat{o}\}}^{(l)}] = 1/(\lambda N_M)$. The final step is to combine all these terms and re-formulize Eq. 5.13 as

$$E[t_o^{(l)}] \approx \left(T_{wait} + 1/(\lambda N_M)\right) \mathrm{EXP}\left(\lambda \sum_{M_j \in M \backslash M_{\hat{o}}} T_{\{bp,j\}}^{(l)}\right)$$
$$+ T_{\{vn,o\}}^{(l)} + T_{\{global,o\}}^{(l)} \tag{5.13}$$

which is convex with respect to λ. Therefore, the optimal block generation rate λ^* is derived from the first-order necessary condition.

The accuracy of the above result with the synchronous approximation is validated by comparing the simulated λ^* without the approximation in the following section.

5.3   Decentralized Privacy-Preserving Protocols

This section presents the proposed decentralized privacy mechanism in edge computing built upon FL-Block. In Fig. 5.4, the network of edge servers is referred as distributed hash table (*DHT*). End devices communicate with edge servers through various provided services.

5.3.1   Hybrid identity

The traditional blockchain identity uses a naive anonymous mechanism. By using a public key, every end device can generate an unlimited number of pseudo-identities

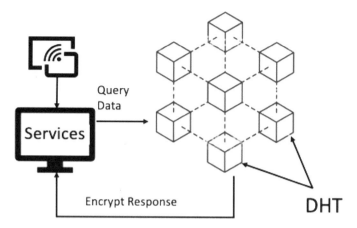

Fig. 5.4 Decentralized privacy in edge computing based on FL-block

if necessary. To extend it to our model, we devise a novel *hybrid identity*. This hybrid identity is a form of personalization of identities. When it is shared to different end devices or edge servers, the owner has full access to it while the other parties have limited access according to specific requirements.

In Algorithm 3, we illustrate an instance of a sole end device identity owner (u_o) and two guest end devices, namely identity recipients (u_g). The identity contains generating key-pairs for the sole owner and two guests. In addition, a symmetric key is required to both encrypt and decrypt the data. In this way, this data is restricted to the other end devices in edge computing. The hybrid identity is defined by a 4-tuple as Eq. 5.14.

Algorithm 3 Hybrid identity generation and memory of blockchain

---

Input: u_o, u_{g_1}, and u_{g_2};
Output: $\text{pk}_{sig_i}^{u_o,u_{g_i}}$, $\text{pk}_{sig_i}^{u_{g_i},u_o}$, $\text{sk}_{enc_i}^{u_o,u_{g_i}}$;
 1: u_o execusions;
 2: $(\text{pk}_{sig_i}^{u_o,u_{g_i}}, \text{sk}_{sig_i}^{u_o,u_{g_i}}) \leftarrow G_{sig}()$;
 3: $\text{sk}_{enc_i}^{u_o,u_{g_i}} \leftarrow G_{enc}()$;
 4: u_o shares $\text{pk}_{sig_i}^{u_o,u_{g_i}}$, $\text{sk}_{enc_i}^{u_o,u_{g_i}}$ to u_{g_1} and u_{g_2};
 5: u_{g_1} execusions;
 6: $(\text{pk}_{sig_i}^{u_{g_i},u_o}, \text{sk}_{sig_i}^{u_{g_i},u_o}) \leftarrow G_{sig}()$;
 7: u_{g_1} shares $\text{pk}_{sig_i}^{u_o,u_{g_i}}$ to u_{g_2} and other u_{g_i}s;
 8: u_{g_2} execusions;
 9: $(\text{pk}_{sig_i}^{u_{g_i},u_o}, \text{sk}_{sig_i}^{u_{g_i},u_o}) \leftarrow G_{sig}()$;
10: u_{g_2} shares $\text{pk}_{sig_i}^{u_o,u_{g_i}}$ to u_{g_1} and other u_{g_i}s;
11: All users have $(\text{pk}_{sig_i}^{u_o,u_{g_i}}, \text{pk}_{sig_i}^{u_{g_i},u_o}, \text{sk}_{enc_i}^{u_o,u_{g_i}})$.

$$\text{Hybrid}_{u,s}^{(public)} = (\text{pk}_{sig_1}^{u_o,u_{g_1}}, \text{pk}_{sig_2}^{u_o,u_{g_2}}, \text{pk}_{sig_1}^{u_{g_1},u_o}, \text{pk}_{sig_2}^{u_{g_2},u_o}) \tag{5.14}$$

Analogically, the integrated hybrid identity will be a 10-tuple, but we use $i|i = 1, 2$ as an index to simplify it to a 5-tuple as Equ. 5.15.

$$\text{Hybrid}_{u,s} = (\text{pk}_{sig_i}^{u_o,u_{g_i}}, \text{sk}_{sig_i}^{u_o,u_{g_i}}, \text{pk}_{sig_i}^{u_{g_i},u_o}, \text{sk}_{sig_i}^{u_{g_i},u_o}, \text{sk}_{enc_i}^{u_o,u_{g_i}}) \tag{5.15}$$

In term of blockchain memory, let BM be the memory space. We have BM : $0, 1^{256} \rightarrow 0, 1^N$ where $N >> 256$ and it is sufficient to store large data files. Blockchain is like an account book containing a list of model updates with a timestamp. The first two outputs in a model update encode the 256-bit memory address pointer along with some auxiliary meta-data. The other outputs are leveraged to build the serialized document. If $L[k]$ is queried, the model update with the up-to-date timestamp will be returned. This setting allows insert, delete, and update operations.

We define the policy P_u as a series of permissions that an end device v can gain from a specific service. For instance, if v needs to read, update, and delete a dataset, then $P_v = read, update, delete$. Any data could be safely stored as service will not break the protocols and label the data incorrectly. In addition, the service can easily observe the anomaly of end devices since all changes are visible.

5.3.2   Accessional Functions

Two accessional functions are necessary in this case, including Parse(x) and Verify(pk_{sig}^k, x_p). Parse(x) continuously passes the arguments to a specific transaction. Verify(pk_{sig}^k, x_p) help verify the permissions of end devices. The protocol of verify function is shown in Algorithm 4.

Algorithm 4 Permission verification

Input: Verify(pk_{sig}^k, x_p);
Output: Verification Index s;
 1: Initialize $s = 0$;
 2: Initialize $a_{policy} = H(\text{pk}_{sig}^k)$;
 3: **if** $BM[a_{policy}] \neq \emptyset$ **then then**
 4:    $\text{pk}_{sig_i}^{u_o,u_{g_i}}, \text{pk}_{sig_i}^{u_{g_i},u_o}, P_{u_o,u_{g_i}} = \text{Parce}(BM[a_{policy}])$;
 5:    **if** $\text{pk}_{sig}^k == \text{pk}_{sig_i}^{u_{g_i},u_o}$ **or then**
 6:      ($\text{pk}_{sig}^k == \text{pk}_{sig_i}^{u_{g_i},u_o}$ **and** $x_p \in P_{u_o,u_{g_i}}$) **then**;
 7:      $s = 1$;
 8:    **end if**
 9: **end if**
10: **return: Verification Index** s.

5.3.3 Access Control and Data Load

In this subsection, we show more detailed protocols of the proposed blockchain model. When a model update A_{access} is recorded, Algorithm 5 is executed by the nodes inside the network. Analogically, when a model update A_{data} is recorded, Pro. 4 is executed by the nodes.

As A_{access} is used to conduct access control management, it can change the permissions of end devices granted by the service. This is accomplished by sending the policy $P_{u_o,u_{g_i}}$. If the service wants to revoke all the access permissions, the policy will be $P_{u_o,u_{g_i}}(\emptyset)$. If it is the first time to send a A_{access} with a new hybrid identity, the A_{access} will be recorded as an end device signing up to a service.

Analogously, A_{data} will manage the data manipulation operations such as read, write, update, or delete. With the assistance of the Verify() function, only the service of edge severs or the permitted end devices can access the differentially private data. In Algorithm 6, we access the distributed hash table like a normal hash table. In real-world scenarios, these instructions bring about some off-chain network messages which are being sent to the distributed hash table.

Algorithm 5 Access control management

Input: Access(pk_{sig}^k, m);
Output: Access Control Index s;
  1: Initialize $s = 0$;
  2: Initialize $\text{pk}_{sig_i}^{u_o,u_{g_i}}, \text{pk}_{sig_i}^{u_{g_i},u_o}, P_{u_o,u_{g_i}} = \text{Parce}(m)$;
  3: **if** $\text{pk}_{sig}^k == \text{pk}_{sig_i}^{u_{g_i},u_o}$ **then then**
  4:       $L[H(\text{pk}_{sig}^k)] = m$;
  5:       $s = 1$;
  6: **end if**
  7: **return:** s.

5.3.4 Discussion

We have some following assumptions in this work. The first one is on the blockchain, which is tamper-proof. This requires a large enough network to avoid untrusted end devices taking over it. The second one is that end devices can properly secure their keys during the operations, for example, using some secure services from edge servers. From here, we will illustrate how the system can protect adversaries from tampering the data stored in a blockchain network. In this scenario, we take less consideration on adversaries modifying protocols or steal personal sensitive information.

In this model, only the services have full control over the sensitive data. An adversary can hardly pretend to be an end device or corrupt the whole network since the blockchain is fully decentralized. In addition, digital signatures are required for

---

Algorithm 6 Data load and storage

Input: DATA(pk_{sig}^{k}, m);
Output: Proper Data Manipulation;
1: Initialize $c, x_p, rw = \text{Parse}(m)$;
2: **if** Verify$(\text{pk}_{sig}^{k}, x_p) = \text{TRUE}$ **then then**
3:      **if** $\text{pk}_{sig}^{k} == \text{pk}_{sig_i}^{u_{g_i}, u_o}$ **then then**
4:          $\text{pk}_{sig_i}^{u_o, u_{g_i}}, \text{pk}_{sig_i}^{u_{g_i}, u_o}, P_{u_o, u_{g_i}} = \text{Parce}(L[H(\text{pk}_{sig}^{u_o, u_{g_i}})])$;
5:          $a_{x_p} = H(\text{pk}_{sig}^{u_o, u_{g_i}} || x_p)$;
6:          **if** $rw = 0$ **then then**
7:              $h_c = H(c)$;
8:              $L[a_{x_p}] = L[a_{x_p}] \cup h_c$;
9:              $ds[h_c] = c$;
10:             **return:** h_c;
11:         **end if**
12:     **else if** $c \in L[a_{x_p}]$ **then**
13:         **return:** $ds[h_c]$;
14:     **end if**
15: **end if**
16: **return:** $\emptyset$.

---

model updates. Therefore, we hold that adversaries are not able to fabricate digital signatures or take control of the majority of the network (over 50%). Furthermore, an adversary cannot poison the data because it is stored off-chain rather on the public ledger. There are only pointers information encrypted with a hash function inside a public ledger.

Even if we consider the case that an adversary controls one or some of the nodes in the DHT network, the adversary cannot learn anything about the data. The rationale behind this is that the data is encrypted with keys that no other nodes have access. The worst case is that the adversary gains the authority and compromises a few local copies of the data, the system can still recover it since there are abundant replications distributed across the whole network.

Last but not least, the hybrid identity mechanism ensures that there is only a tiny probability that the data is poisoned because this requires the acquisition of both signing key and encryption-decryption key. If the adversaries happen to steal one of the keys, the sensitive data is still safe. In practice, we can also personalize the hybrid identity so that the compromization is restricted for the adversaries. A good instance would be different keys for a certain volume of records.

5.4   Performance Evaluation

In this section, we testify the superiority of the proposed FL-Block model in term of privacy protection and efficiency. We simulate an edge computing environment and create a blockchain network. Based on this, we conduct experiments on machine learning tasks using real-world datasets of large scale.

5.4.1 Simulation Environment Description

The simulated edge computing environment is implemented on the cellular network of an urban microcell. It is consisted of 3 edge servers, and $N_v = 50$ end devices, on a single workstation. The three edge servers are located at the center of the cell with a radius of 3 kilometers, while the end devices are distributed with a normal distribution in this cell.

To model the wireless communications, we introduce the LTE networks with a popular urban channel model, which is defined in the ITU-R M.2135-1 Micro NLOS model of a hexagonal cell layout [15]. The transmission power and antenna gain of the edge server and end devices are set to be 30 dBm and 0 dBi, respectively, for simplicity. Carrier frequency is set to 2.5 GHz, and the antenna heights of the edge servers and end devices are set to 11 m and 1 m, correspondingly. We use a practical bandwidth limitation, namely 20 RBs, which corresponds to a bandwidth of 1.8 MHz. This is assigned to an end device in each time slot of 0.5 ms. We employ a throughput model based on the Shannon capacity with a certain loss used in [16], in which $\Delta = 1.6$ and $\rho_{max} = 4.8$. With these initialized settings, the mean and maximum throughputs of client θ_k are 1.4 and 8.6 Mb/s, which are practical and feasible in LTE networks. The details of the simulation results are summarized in Table 5.1 for clarity.

From the aforementioned model, we obtain the throughput and consider it as the average throughput. This throughput is leveraged to derive t in the end device selection phase. We assume the network environment is stable and thereby the federated learning process will not be impacted by network connectivity issues. In this way, we can regard the average throughput as stable outputs. To better simulate the real-world scenarios, we take a small variation of short-term throughput at the scheduled update and upload into consideration. The throughput will be sampled from the Gaussian distribution when the models' updates are shared between end devices and edge servers. The Gaussian distribution is defined by the average throughput and its $r\%$ value as the mean and standard deviation, respectively.

Table 5.1 Simulation parameters overview

Item	Value/description
LTE network	ITU-R M.2135-1 Micro NLOS
Transmission power	30 dBm
Antenna gain	0 dBm
Antenna heights of the edge servers	11 m
Antenna heights of the end devices	1 m
Bandwidth	1.8 MHz
Time slot	0.5 ms
Δ	1.6
ρ_{max}	4.8
Mean throughputs	1.4 Mb/s
Maximum throughputs	8.6 Mb/s

5.4.2 Global Models and Corresponding Updates

In order to guarantee the output's accuracy, the **IID** setting is considered, in which each end device will randomly sample a specific amount of data from the raw dataset.

We implement a classic CNN as the global model for all tasks. In particular, FL-Block contains six 3*3 convolution layers, including 2*32, 2*64, and 2*128 channels. In each of the channel, it is activated by ReLU and batch normalized, while every pair of them is followed by 2*2 max pooling. In addition, the six channels are followed by three fully connected layers, including 382 and 192 units with ReLU activation and another 10 units activated by soft-max. In this case, the model will approximately have 3.6 million parameters for Fashion-MINIST and 4.6 million parameters for CIFAR-10. The size of D_m are 14.4 and 18.3 mb, respectively, while the data type is set to be 32-bit float. Although some other deep models will have better performances, they are not the focus of this model and is not considered.

The hyper-parameters of updating global models are initialized as follows. The mini-batch size is 40. The number of epochs in each round is 40. The initial learning rate of stochastic gradient descent updates is 0.30. The learning rate decay is 0.95. We simply model the computation capability of each end device as how many data samples it could train to further update the global model. There might be slight fluctuation due to some other tasks on this end device. We randomly decide the average capability of each end device from the interval [10, 100], which will be used in the client selection phase. Consequently, the update time in client selection phase averagely ranges from 5 to 500 s. The computation capability depends on the Gaussian distribution in both the scheduled update phase and the upload phase. The Gaussian distribution is defined by the average throughput and its $r\%$ value as the mean and standard deviation, respectively. The range is considered to be reasonable since the workstation needs 4 s considering one single update with one single GPU. They may require longer update time up to 100 times if the mobile devices have a weaker computation power. Empirically, we set T_{final} to 400 s and T_{round} to 3 s.

In Tables 5.2 and 5.3, we illustrate the evaluation results with the *IID* settings in terms of ToA and accuracy. Each method is executed for 10 times and the ToA and accuracy scores are measured from the averaging perspective. In term of ToA, FL-Block has excellent performances on both tasks. The architecture is sufficient to show the efficiency of the newly designed protocols under resource-limited settings. However, the best accuracy is not the target in FL-Block. The original federated learning without deadline limitations achieved accuracies of 0.80 and 0.92 for CIFAR-10 and Fashion-MNIST, respectively. The obtained accuracies are comparable to the performances of FL-Block. Two traditional major concerns, which are the uncertainty of throughput and computation capabilities, do not have a significant impact on the FL-Block's performances.

Table 5.2 Evaluation results of CIFAR-10

Indexes	ToA(0.5)	ToA(0.75)	Accuracy
$T_{round} = 3$ s (r = 0%)	24.5	122.3	0.76
$T_{round} = 3$ s (r = 10%)	26.8	136.1	0.74
$T_{round} = 3$ s (r = 20%)	30.2	182.5	0.72
$T_{round} = 1$ s (r = 0%)	NAN	NAN	0.50
$T_{round} = 5$ s (r = 0%)	45.1	178.5	0.77
$T_{round} = 10$ s (r = 0%)	80.7	312.5	0.75

ToA(x) (**in seconds**) is the time costed to reach a specific testing classification accuracy of x. The performance upgrades with the decrease of ToA
Accuracy: it denotes the accuracy value for the final iteration

Table 5.3 Evaluation results of fashion-MINIST

Indexes	ToA(0.5)	ToA(0.75)	Accuracy
$T_{round} = 3$ s (r = 0%)	15.6	39.3	0.89
$T_{round} = 3$ s (r = 10%)	16.6	40.2	0.88
$T_{round} = 3$ s (r = 20%)	17.3	45.5	0.91
$T_{round} = 1$ s (r = 0%)	5.4	86.4	0.87
$T_{round} = 5$ s (r = 0%)	25.1	60.7	0.92
$T_{round} = 10$ s (r = 0%)	58.2	110.8	0.93

ToA(x) (**in seconds**) is the time costed to reach a specific testing classification accuracy of x. The performance upgrades with the decrease of ToA
Accuracy: it denotes the accuracy value for the final iteration.

From the aspect of the impact of T_{round}, we evaluate the changes in the classification accuracy and ToA. As shown in Figs. 5.5, 5.6, and 5.7, and Table 5.3, FL-Block on fashion MNIST has different values of deadline T_{round} while maintaining T_{final} constant. It is observable that the value of T_{round} should be in a proper range without being too large or too small. Because of the smaller number of aggregation phases, longer deadlines like 20 s with FL-Block involved numerous end devices in each round, which leads to extremely limited performances. From the other angle, if we set a short deadline like 1 s to limit the number of end devices accessible in each round, the classification performances are also degraded in an unexpected way. Therefore, a possible promising method of selecting T_{round} would be dynamically changing it to align an abundant amount of end devices in each iteration.

5.4.3 Evaluation on Convergence and Efficiency

From the perspective of convergence and efficiency, FL-Block can achieve convergence at different learning rates. Intuitively, greater learning rate results in faster convergence, which is also testified with the evaluation results. As illustrated in Fig. 5.8, FL-Block reaches convergences when data size is moderate, which means the scalability is excellent. Even if the data size is great, the model can still achieve

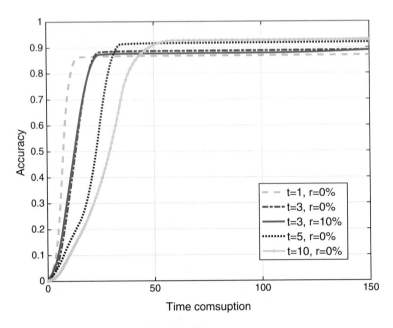

Fig. 5.5 Effects of different values of deadline T_{round}: accuracy

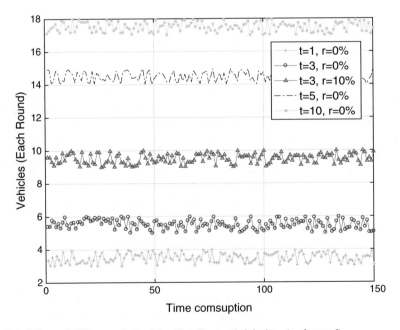

Fig. 5.6 Effects of different values of deadline T_{round}: end devices (each round)

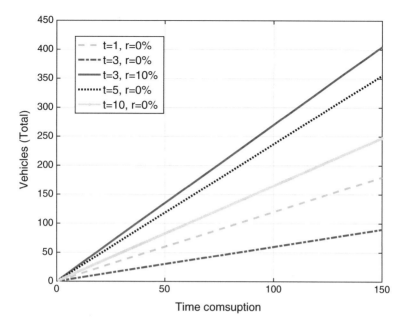

Fig. 5.7 Effects of different values of deadline T_{round}: end devices (total)

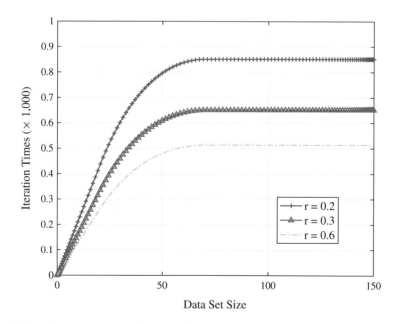

Fig. 5.8 Iteration convergence vs. increase of data size

fast convergence. The convergence value of FL-Block is 0.69 when the learning rate is 0.6. It is significant superior comparing to the other two ones, which converges at 0.51 and 0.41, respectively. Therefore, FL-Block fully meets the requirements of big data scenarios, in particular, edge computing applications.

5.4.4 Evaluation on Blockchain

In Figs. 5.9 and 5.10, we show how the block generation rate λ influences the average learning completion latency of FL-Block. We can tell that the latency is convex-shaped over the generation rate λ and simultaneously decreasing with the SNRs in Fig. 5.11. From Fig. 5.12, we show the minimized average learning completion latency time based on the optimal block generation rate λ^*. The value of latency time derived from the proposition is greater than the simulated minimum latency by up to 2.0% .

Figures 5.11 and 5.12 illustrate the FL-Block's scalability in terms of the numbers N_M and N_V of miners and end devices, respectively. In Fig. 5.11, the average learning completion latency is computed for $N_M = 5$ and $N_M = 10$ with and without the malfunction of miners. To capture the malfunction, Gaussian noise complying with $N \sim (-0.1; 0.1)$ is added to the aggregated local model updates of each miner with a probability of 0.5. In the scenario of without malfunction,

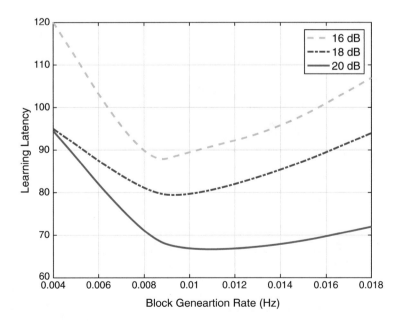

Fig. 5.9 Block generation: λ

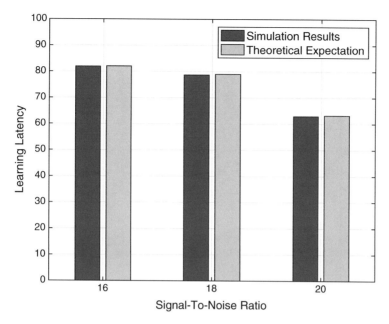

Fig. 5.10   Block generation: λ^*

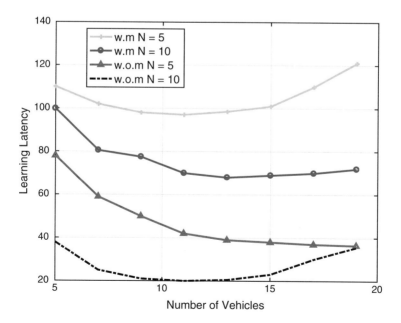

Fig. 5.11   Learning latency: w.m: with malfunction; w.o.m: without malfunction

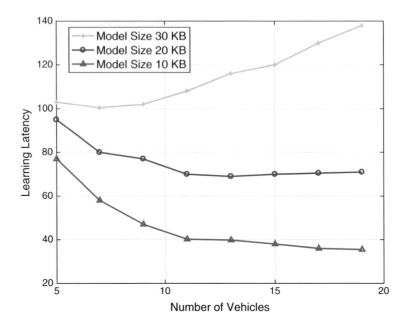

Fig. 5.12 Learning latency: model size

the latency increases with the increase of N_M because of the resource consumption in block propagation delays and cross-verification operation. However, this is not always the case when there is malfunction involved. In FL-Block, the malfunction of each miner only impacts on the global model update of the corresponding end device. This kind of distortion could be eliminated by federating with other non-tempering end devices and miners. On this account, the increase of N_M may result in a shorter latency, which is testified in the provided evaluation results, for instance, $N_M = 20$ with malfunction.

With Fig. 5.11, we show that a latency-optimal number N_V of end devices are identified. A greater value of N_V enables the usage of a larger number of data samples. However, this will increase the size of each block as well as the delays of block exchange, which brings about the aforementioned convex-shaped latency. It increases each block size such as communication payload. Therefore, it leads to higher block exchange delays and consequently resulting in the convex-shaped latency concerning N_V. That is why a reasonable end device selection can potentially reduce the expected latency.

Lastly, Fig. 5.12 shows that the latency increases with local model size δ_m of each end device, which is intuitive but vital. For this reason, it calls for novel model compression mechanisms, which will also be part of our future work.

5.4.5 Evaluation on Poisoning Attack Resistance

In FL-Block, the poisoning attack could be resisted in a high-confidence way because of the nature of blockchain and the enhanced protocols we propose. In this simulation, we compare the performance of FL-Block with both classic blockchain and federated learning. The assumption here is the initialization phase of the proposed blockchain network where blocks and miners are small enough to allow these attacks to breakthrough Blockchain and thereby poisoning attack is possible to manipulate the data in a malicious way.

In Fig. 5.13, we use semi-logarithmic coordinate system to compare the performances of the three models. With the increase of the adversary's hash-rate, more turbulence will be there for all three models. However, only when the hash-rate reaches a threshold, the adversary can launch a poisoning attack to the data under the protection of Blockchain. This only happens when the number of blocks is 10 in this simulation. If there are more blocks, it takes much more time as the time consumption increases in an exponential manner.

Figure 5.14 shows how much an adversary needs to break through the protection in regarding to different blocks. It looks like in a linearly tendency as the y axis is presented by a semi-logarithmic axis. That means the hash-rate increases in an exponential manner as well. It requires $10^{13}+$ when the block reaches 30. As the difficulty of generating a block increases over time, it provides higher and higher protection when a blockchain develops.

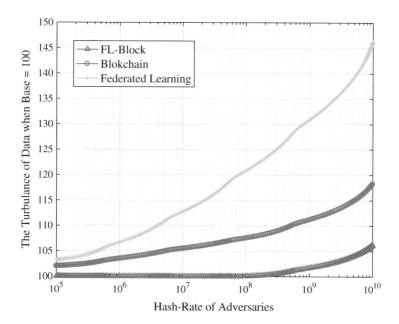

Fig. 5.13 Poisoning attack resistance performance: comparison among three models

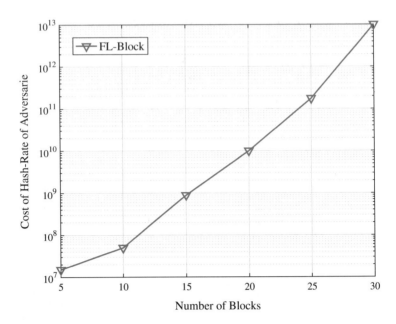

Fig. 5.14 Poisoning attack resistance performance: successful attack requirements based on number of blocks

5.5   Summary

In this chapter, we propose a novel blockchain-enabled federated learning model to solve the identified issues in edge computing. End devices upload the local updates to the edge servers, where the global updates will be generated and stored. Since only the pointer of the global updates is saved on-chain while a distributed hash table (DHT) is used to save to data, the block generation efficiency could be guaranteed. With a hybrid identity generation, comprehensive verification, access control, and off-chain data storage and retrieve, FL-Block enables decentralized privacy protection while preventing single point failure. Moreover, the poisoning attack could be eliminated from the aspect of edge servers. Extensive evaluation results on real-world datasets are presented to show the superiority of FL-Block.

References

1. L. Ma, X. Liu, Q. Pei, Y. Xiang, Privacy-preserving reputation management for edge computing enhanced mobile crowdsensing. IEEE Trans. Serv. Comput. **12**(5), 786–799 (2018)
2. M.A. Ferrag, L.A. Maglaras, A. Ahmim, Privacy-preserving schemes for ad hoc social networks: a survey. IEEE Commun. Surv. Tutor. **19**(4), 3015–3045 (2017)

3. Y. Qu, S. Yu, L. Gao, W. Zhou, S. Peng, A hybrid privacy protection scheme in cyber-physical social networks. IEEE Trans. Comput. Soc. Syst. **5**(3), 773–784 (2018)

4. Y. Qu, S. Yu, W. Zhou, S. Peng, G. Wang, K. Xiao, Privacy of things: emerging challenges and opportunities in wireless internet of things. IEEE Wirel. Commun. **25**(6), 91–97 (2018)

5. H. Zhu, F. Wang, R. Lu, F. Liu, G. Fu, H. Li, Efficient and privacy-preserving proximity detection schemes for social applications. IEEE Internet Things J. **5**(4), 2947–2957 (2018)

6. M.M.E.A. Mahmoud, N. Saputro, P. Akula, K. Akkaya, Privacy-preserving power injection over a hybrid AMI/LTE smart grid network. IEEE Internet of Things J. **4**(4), 870–880 (2017)

7. J. Hu, L.-L. Yang, L. Hanzo, Energy-efficient cross-layer design of wireless mesh networks for content sharing in online social networks. IEEE Trans. Veh. Technol. **66**(9), 8495–8509 (2017)

8. Cynthia Dwork, Differential privacy, in *Proceedings of ICALP 2006*, Venice, July 10–14 (2006), pp. 1–12

9. L. Lyu, K. Nandakumar, B.I.P. Rubinstein, J. Jin, J. Bedo, M. Palaniswami, PPFA: privacy preserving fog-enabled aggregation in smart grid. IEEE Trans. Ind. Inf. **14**(8), 3733–3744 (2018)

10. L. Ma, Q. Pei, L. Zhou, H. Zhu, L. Wang, Y. Ji, Federated data cleaning: collaborative and privacy-preserving data cleaning for edge intelligence. IEEE Internet Things J. **8**(8), 6757–6770 (2020)

11. R. Lu, X. Lin, H. Zhu, P.-H. Ho, X. Shen, ECPP: efficient conditional privacy preservation protocol for secure vehicular communications, in *INFOCOM 2008. 27th IEEE International Conference on Computer Communications, Joint Conference of the IEEE Computer and Communications Societies*, 13–18 April 2008, Phoenix, AZ, pp. 1229–1237

12. B. McMahan, D. Ramage, Federated learning: collaborative machine learning without centralized training data. Google Research Blog, 3 (2017)

13. S. Samarakoon, M. Bennis, W. Saad, M. Debbah, Distributed federated learning for ultra-reliable low-latency vehicular communications (2018). CoRR abs/1807.08127

14. H. Kim, J. Park, M. Bennis, S.-L. Kim, On-device federated learning via blockchain and its latency analysis (2018). CoRR abs/1808.03949

15. M Series, Guidelines for evaluation of radio interface technologies for imt-advanced. Report ITU, 638 (2009)

16. M.R. Akdeniz, Y. Liu, M.K. Samimi, S. Sun, S. Rangan, T.S. Rappaport, E. Erkip, Millimeter wave channel modeling and cellular capacity evaluation. IEEE J. Select. Areas Commun. **32**(6), 1164–1179 (2014)

Chapter 6
Conclusion and Future Research Issues

6.1 Conclusion

The research presented in this monograph mainly focuses on privacy preservation issues in the edge computing paradigm in terms of data utility, privacy protection level, and efficiency of privacy preservation. This monograph consists of five chapters. We first study the current research backgrounds of edge computing and its privacy issues by analyzing the privacy challenges that exist in the edge computing paradigm. According to the challenges, this monograph focuses on the improvement and analysis of the overall paradigm in edge computing at the beginning. Second, based on the solid foundation that was developed, we discuss context-aware privacy issues at the end by proposing a MDP-based mechanism with SARSA reinforcement learning capabilities to archive optimal tradeoffs while enhancing the data utility and privacy level. Furthermore, we concentrate on privacy issues for location-aware applications by proposing a dual-scheme privacy protection model against multiple attacking scenarios. Moreover, we propose a novel decentralized blockchain-enabled federated learning (FL-Block) scheme which allows privacy-preserving local learning updates of end devices exchanges with blockchain-based global learning model.

In summary, the data optimizations and privacy issues in edge computing have been identified in each chapter. The solutions are proposed and highly focused on both context-aware and location-aware application. The overall performance of edge computing is also recognized. The proposed methods can significantly increase the reliabilities and manageabilities. Furthermore, according to the levelled up performance results, we target on the solutions that aim to protect the data privacy with guaranteed privacy level and data utilities. Iteration time and QoS are also ensured in our proposed solutions.

© The Author(s), under exclusive license to Springer Nature Singapore Pte Ltd. 2021   111
L. Gao et al., *Privacy-Preserving in Edge Computing*, Wireless Networks,
https://doi.org/10.1007/978-981-16-2199-4_6

6.2 Future Work

Although the proposed methods improved data handling performance and privacy issues from various application scenarios in edge computing, there are a few challenges that need to be addressed in future work. This section discusses open issues and challenges as future extensions of the presented work.

Performance Analyze in SD-Enabled Edge Computing
We discussed the big data performance issues in edge computing by integrating SDN, and the proposed framework was proven by extensive experiments. To determine the priorities of users, devices, facilities, hardware and the data generated by IoT devices in an edge network, popular systems for personalization, optimization, and customization, such as recommender systems, can help the DSL to provide more dynamic and optimized solutions for improving the user experience and assisting in resolving data sparsity issues. However, in this architecture, such recommender systems should not only serve the end users but also provide recommendations regarding the communication among edge nodes and between the edge network and the cloud. For edge-to-edge recommendation, a recommender system can provide suggestions regarding the quantity and quality of edge nodes needed to constitute a virtualized clustered network to efficiently improve system performance. Such a system can also recommend whether and what data should be cached or stored in the edge nodes. At the edge-to-user level, similar to a traditional recommender system, such a system can provide the most relevant or feasible content to users based on a system analysis of user habits and relevant information provided in the same edge node. For example, to determine which stores discount information should be recommended to a user, such a recommender system can synthetically analyze the user movement path among the geographically distributed edge nodes, web browsing information, and other relevant information generated by the users' devices. A recommender system can also guide the user in choosing between connections to the edge network and the cloud network to achieve better performance; for example, if the calculation limit of the existing edge network is exceeded, the system can recommend that the user connect to the cloud to enable more comprehensive computing. Overall, such a content recommendation solution provided by the DSL SD controller can improve the edge network performance and the user experience. Furthermore, in big data, the recommendation system also contains a massive quantity of user data and may cause privacy leakage during the process.

Advanced Privacy-Preserving Scheme in Edge Computing
In Chap. 3, we proposed a context-aware privacy-preserving model on the foundation of MDP to achieve optimal tradeoff. The proposed model improved data utility and reserved the privacy protection level from the tradeoff. We will continue to pursue the extension and generalization of the current model by analyzing the convergence with limited computing power. We plan to utilize deep learning algorithms to identify a more accurate solution with higher protection. In the future,

energy efficiency during data collection in a large-scale edge computing network is also a possible promising direction.

We also plan to research further for data privacy preservation on both location-aware and context-aware applications by analyzing different attack models such as background knowledge attacks and collusion attacks. In addition, further consideration includes energy consumption, iteration time, and data utilities. Reinforcement learning is an excellent tool for obtaining better training models on large-scale datasets for the edge computing paradigm. Moreover, we are preparing to conduct a more comprehensive study on the current model and topic to extend overall performances.

Blockchain-Empowered Privacy-Preserving Edge Computing
With the fast proliferation of edge devices, the communication overhead is exponentially increasing between edge devices and cloud servers, which drags down the performance of edge computing systems. Thus, edge computing becomes gradually autonomous. Besides, data falsification has been a long-lasting issue of edge computing. Therefore, blockchain-empowered edge computing is fast emerging to fill the above gaps. As an underlying architecture, blockchain allows the edge devices to make local decisions via consensus algorithm while several other advantageous features jointly contribute to the security improvement, such as cross validation.

However, privacy leakage issues become even severe when blockchain is involved. Usually, the data is publicly accessible to all nodes, in this case, the edge devices. This means a trusted data curator no longer exists. Therefore, it is essential to sanitize the raw data before sharing while maintaining the data utility and cross verifiability. To make this feasible, there are two potential solutions.

The first solution is using lightweight attribute-based homomorphic encryption specially designed for blockchain-empowered edge computing. The raw data is encrypted before sharing to the other edge devices, while the edge devices with required attributes are able to operate on the encrypted data, such as aggregation or verification. The data utility is fully maintained while the verification could be achieved as part of the design of the lightweight attribute-based homomorphic encryption.

The second solution is to devise a modified personalized differential privacy model. Existing differential privacy model may not fit into this scenario directly due to the low data utility and the assumption of a distribution such as Laplace distribution or Gaussian distribution. To improve it, it is possible to use machine learning based methods. For instance, it is possible to use generative adversarial network to achieve differential privacy. By adding one more condition (compliance with differential privacy), the improved differential privacy has a potential to largely improve the data utility while removing the assumption of distributions. Besides, if the privacy protection level is personalized based the community, the verification is also achievable within the community. In this case, the privacy can be preserved in blockchain-empowered edge computing systems.

Printed in the United States
by Baker & Taylor Publisher Services